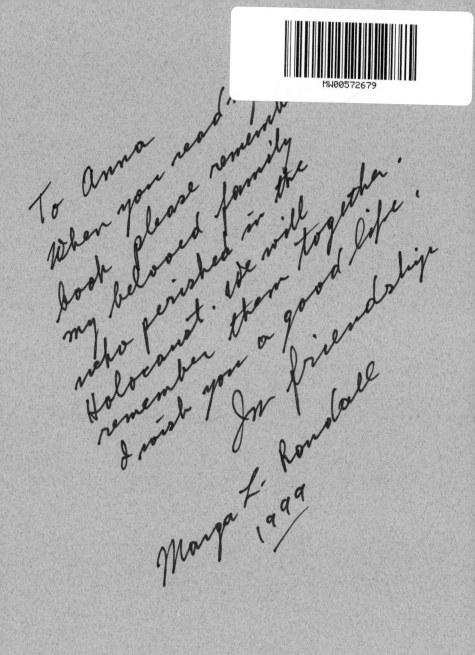

To Anna

When you read this
book please remember
my beloved family
who perished in the
Holocaust. We will
remember them together.
I wish you a good life.

In friendship

Marga L. Randall
1999

HOW BEAUTIFUL
WE ONCE WERE

Marga Silbermann Randall

HOW BEAUTIFUL WE ONCE WERE

A REMEMBRANCE OF THE HOLOCAUST AND BEYOND

CATHEDRAL PUBLISHING

PITTSBURGH, PENNSYLVANIA

Published by Cathedral Publishing, Pittsburgh, PA 15260
Copyright ©1998 Cathedral Publishing
All rights reserved.
http://www.pitt.edu/~ondemand
Manufactured in the United States of America
Printed on acid-free paper
Cover Design: Craig Seder
Book Design: Kathy Boykowycz
ISBN: 1-887969-06-3

Libray of Congress Cataloging-in-Publication Data

Randall, Marga Silbermann, 1930–
    How beautiful we once were : a remembrance of the Holocaust and
beyond / Marga Silbermann Randall.
        p.   cm.
    Includes bibliographical references.
    ISBN 1-887969-06-3 (alk. paper)
    1. Randall, Marga Silbermann, 1930–   . 2. Jews—Germany—
–Schermbeck--Biography.   3. Jewish Children in the Holocaust-
-Germany--Schermbeck--Personal narratives.   4. Schermbeck (Germany)-
-Ethnic relations.   I. Title.
DS135.G5R267   1998
940.53'18'092--dc21   97-48045
                                                                    CIP

CONTENTS

FOREWORD

The town of Schermbeck, Germany is so small that it is difficult to find on a map. By the 1930s, the Jewish community there had shrunk to only a handful. So why write about such a tiny segment who suffered persecution and annihilation then? Precisely as this is a microcosm, Marga Randall's memories of that tragic period are important. Here we see persecution, destruction, and deportation in an intimate, highly personal setting where every person knew everyone else. We are provided with a different set of insights into the horrors of the Holocaust as felt by the victims and as remembered by the townspeople.

The Jews in Schermbeck felt isolated and cut off as they did not have the support of larger communities, which had their own problems. The general German population was frightened by the Nazis in their midst and by outsiders who came to the community and enforced the anti-Semitic decrees. No local leadership was willing to take a courageous stand and we hear from ordinary folks — who were neighbors to Jews — about those who protested directly and indirectly, their reminiscences presented clearly and forcefully.

Marga Randall has woven the events of her early childhood into a broader picture of her entire family, the members of the older generation and middle generation, who faced persecution or flight to a safe haven as best they could. She has shown us all the juxtaposition with later post-World War II visits to Germany and the recollections of both those who survived the persecutions and those who lived through the war in Germany. The excuses, altered memories, as well as regrets are shown in this slim volume on a very human small-town scale.

The interspersion of photographs has added greatly to this recollection as they show us the people involved, both Jewish and non-Jewish. As we search their faces and probe their demeanor, we can place the events into their proper setting and begin to come to terms with the issues raised by this the greatest tragedy of the 20th century.

Marga Randall's story contains no surprises; there is nothing which we did not know. No unusual adventures or dramas have been related. It is precisely because we are dealing with the very ordinary group of Jews and gentiles tucked away in a half-forgotten community which makes this story significant. Here we have some insights into ordinary people living extraordinary lives. We see their fears and regrets, and a broad unwillingness to react to the plight of neighbors with whom they have lived for many generations. It is the hauntingly ordinary which makes this a fine book.

Dr. Walter Jacob
Rabbi Emeritus
Temple Rodef Shalom

ACKNOWLEDGEMENTS

It was my own dedication to the subject of the Holocaust and my commitment to keep the memory of my beloved family alive that brought me to write about this period in history. I truly needed the encouragement and support of family and friends to show me that I had the potential to write about such an overwhelming topic. I have a debt of gratitude to those close to my heart.

I wish to thank my family, my beloved husband, Jordan, who passed away six years ago, and my three wonderful children, Judy E. McAllister, Robert L. Randall, and Nancy S. Kovach, who then blessed us with three grandchildren, Jennifer L. Kovach, Lyndsay Kovach, and Clayton Jordan McAllister, for their total love, support and gratitude all these years, and my brother, Herbert and my sister, Hilda.

Reverend Wolfgang Bornebusch brought me back to Schermbeck in order to recapture my past and, in doing so, brightened my future. Isaiah Kupperstein, past director of the Pittsburgh Holocaust Center, encouraged me to speak out early on and often brought out the best in me as an educator and writer. The Holocaust survivors, who shared their incredible and often painful memories, made it possible to tell stories so that I might help others understand.

From a spiritual standpoint, Helen Reitmeyer, who remained a loyal friend for many years, listened to my stories and shared ideas; I hope she is still listening from Heaven. Thanks to dear friends Sorlee Chetlin, who is always there for me, and Jeanne Rascoe, who will remain in my thoughts. Gilya G. Schmidt expressed great interest in my work, and her deep sensitivity and understanding helped me beyond words. My friend Rabbi Mark Mahler of the Temple Emanuel gave me strength and guidance along with his blessings, as did Marlis Fengels, who is my loving friend and supporter in Schermbeck.

I wish to thank Frank Lehner, Craig Seder, and Cathedral Publishing for believing in this book and turning it into a reality. Also, Tony Del Prete for his edits and input, as well as Honey Adelsheim who helped me with the initial draft. I could not have done this without Dr. Hedwig O. Pregler teaching me and caring for me when I began my life America, and all my friends who have listened, provided input and inspiration, and encouraged me to continue with what has become my life's work.

This book is dedicated to
my mother, Mutti.
In it I write all the words
she could not speak, give all
the love she had left to give,
feel all of her deep pain
for our own flesh and blood
that Hitler burned.
I will devote my life
to her memory,
so we will never forget.

Hanna Silbermann
c. 1920, Lemfoerde

PROLOGUE

I have written this book simply because I had to. I had a story to tell about my family and the world we lived in and how that world was destroyed so that now all that remains are the memories. It is a story about our family's experience with the Holocaust and how one little girl's search for her past has led to hope for the future.

As a Jewish family living in Germany prior to World War II we were respected members of society, patriotic citizens who fought for their country. We were German Jews, for that is the way we thought of ourselves: German first, Jewish second. We were not Jews living in Germany; we were an integrated part of society. In every way, in our view of the world and our place in it, we were Germans. We felt secure, so when the madness began, to our way of thinking, it had nothing to do with us. Then, one man's evil plot quickly transformed an entire population. We and millions like us were persecuted, effectively wiping out a people, denying our contributions, negating our traditions and defiling our heritage.

The stories captured in this book show how normal our life was in the village of my birth and how rapidly changes came about. Each anecdote is a piece of the puzzle that is my life. Some deal with suffering, some with fascinating coincidences, others are encouraging and many are simply inspiring. But all of them are about people and, to me, people are the only thing that matters.

You will get to know my family: Opa, my anchor in a changing world; my beloved Mutti, with all her strength and love; my dear cousins, Hanna and Ruth; and aunts, uncles, friends and new acquaintances. You will see my village, walk its streets, and glimpse life and landscape as I knew it — and got to know it again.

It is important that these people, places and events continue to live on in spirit and so I have dedicated my life and work to tell the world. They were not brilliant scientists or great leaders. They were just ordinary people who loved one another, harmed no one and, to the best of their ability, served the community in which they lived.

A tragic outgrowth of the Holocaust is the complete loss of family history and tradition. I have made it a part of my life, my very fiber, to preserve these precious stories to be told and retold in the hope that they will never be forgotten.

1 | GOING HOME

Forty-one years to the day after our family had entered the United States, ultimately escaping the oppression of the Nazis, I arrived back in Schermbeck, Germany. I was there to visit the place where my mother was born and raised, where I grew up, and where our synagogue once stood. I would also make a journey to my father's grave. It promised to be a bittersweet experience.

While in Germany I also was to make several presentations, and I was looking forward to the entire experience with great anticipation. Reverend Bornebusch, a good friend, had put together an exhibit, "The Life of the Former Jewish Community in Schermbeck," hoping that the generations of Germans born after the war could better understand how the German Jews had once been an integral part of society. As a survivor of the Holocaust, I had permitted my picture to be included as part of his exhibit, and now I was making the commitment to give support to this man who had made such an effort to keep the memory of Jewish Schermbeckers alive.

It was Monday, June 21, 1982 when I entered the home of Reverend Bornebusch. I was in Schermbeck less than an hour when the phone rang. It was my brother, Herbert, calling from the U.S. with the sad news that Mother had passed away. Suddenly, my event schedule and speaking engagements weren't very important. My mother, always a source of inspiration to me, was gone. I wish that I could have known what suffering she endured, for there were many difficult moments in her life, especially during World War II. My mother could never say no to a request. Inconveniences never set her back. Kind and quiet, she was loved by her friends. To me she was a role model — my role model — to emulate and pattern my life upon. What happened to this gentle woman after her Germany fell apart around her, in fact, after it was torn asunder, and how America, with its strange customs and unfamiliar language became her home, is a story of strength, courage, wisdom and survival common to many Holocaust survivors.

As I tried to fathom the irony in my mother's untimely death, I recalled seeing her the day before I left for Germany. She was wearing a white dress, summer jewelry and shoes to match, a vision of health. We had breakfast together and I taped our conversation, the clanging of utensils in the background and her voice telling me to be careful, to be sure nothing would happen to me. We hugged and kissed and then I waved and threw more kisses to her from our car until I could see her no more.

I last spoke to my mother a week later from Geneva where I had stopped to visit a cousin. I was awakened there at 7 a.m. the morning I was to leave for Schermbeck with the news she was ill and had been hospitalized with a heart problem. My husband, Jordan, told me it wasn't necessary to return right away, it was not serious. But I had an insecure, uneasy feeling and, as our boat drifted along the flowing tears of the Rhine River I wanted only to be with her. As I returned to my mother's birthplace, the birthplace of our family, I prayed but my heart was heavy.

Now I would have to return to Schermbeck alone, without the knowledge that she was there if I needed her. It was frightening that I was making a journey back from where we came, to the very town that harbored such horrific memories of the Nazis, and I shuddered at the thought. Never in my wildest dreams would I think that I would be leaving my family in America to return to Germany. I thought that once we left that Godforsaken place we'd never go back. But there is beauty in Schermbeck, too. And although I wrestled with the haunting visions from my youth, I wanted to see the lake, the town, the people.

Forty-five years had passed since any family member had returned to Schermbeck, and I was so pleased that I could do this for my mother, to say a prayer over my father's grave and have mother's spirit there with me. I had a bronze Star of David cast to place on his stone. And now, consoled by those around me, I wanted to hold her and tell her how much I loved her before she closed her eyes forever. Almost nauseous with grief, I did what I had set out to do. I went to my father's grave and, facing the headstone, I said the memorial prayer, a prayer which I had intended for him, and now, with the news from home, I would say for her. At that moment, in my heart I felt I somehow bonded them together, joined them in some way, and I laid my hand on his grave and scooped some of the earth into a small container that I would later bring home.

That evening, Wolfgang wanted to hear one of my lectures, so I chose one of the three tapes I had with me. As it began to play, I realized it was the last practice speech for the unveiling ceremony, and I heard myself say "I am grateful to be here at this funeral." We were all stunned. I had used the German word *"beerdigung"* meaning funeral instead of *"enthullung"* meaning unveiling. Was it a slip of the tongue or a premonition?

The trip home felt as if I were carrying a heavy weight, a special burden, a leaden emptiness. I went three days without sleep and I was fatigued to the point of exhaustion, but I could not shake the painful realization that my mother was not there for me to talk with any more. I barely remember who paid their respects; I think I was in shock. I could only think of her. At the cemetery, when the memorial service came to an end, I took the earth from my father's grave and placed it upon her casket. In doing so I had returned the earth from her roots in Schermbeck and said good-bye to a valiant survivor of the Holocaust.

Yet, for my mother and father to rest in peace, I must tell their story, a story that mirrors the lives and tragic times of so many Jews who suffered through, and continue to suffer, the atrocities of the Holocaust.

2 | I REMEMBER OUR FAMILY

My mother, Hanna Silbermann, nee Adelsheimer, daughter of Gustav and Emma, was born in Schermbeck, the Rheinland, June 17, 1894. She grew up with three sisters and one brother, married Louis Silbermann in 1918, and moved into the family home in Lemfoerde, an area called Lower Saxony near Onasbruck. That is where my story begins.

It was there, frail and vulnerable, premature and weighing only 2.5 pounds, I was delivered by a midwife on March 20, 1930. I was the last of four children. In those days, loving and nurturing were the only keys to survival, and so I was placed in a cradle, surrounded by hot water bottles around the clock and was fed special goat's milk my father brought from the countryside every day. My body weak, my prognosis not encouraging, my mother stood over me day and night to give me a chance to live. Like a cat with nine lives, this was the first of many battles I would survive.

The early years of my childhood were carefree and I played and sang like any other youngster who felt loved. However, my life changed forever just six days after my fourth birthday. A friend of my father's called to tell him that the Gestapo were coming to arrest him. With the news he fell dead at my feet. I remember that he was laid on a sofa, a white pillow placed beneath his head, and I was whisked off to spend the day with a neighbor. After that we moved in with friends for several weeks and soon after my two brothers went off to learn a trade, my mother became a housekeeper in a grand Jewish home in nearby Dinslaken. I was sent to live in Schermbeck with my mother's sister, Paula, who would raise me according to mother's wishes.

My father's death fractured our family into three groups going in different directions. I know it must have broken my mother's heart to see all of her children leave her side, but it was a common tragedy of the times. Whether it was the shock or a reaction to a heart injury he suffered in the war, I'll never know what killed my father and, in essence, our entire family.

My father, Louis Silbermann (1885–1934), a.k.a. "Taxi Louie"

One thing is for certain, however, he was a casualty of the Holocaust as sure as if they'd gassed him in the showers.

Everyone knew my father as Taxi Louie, a nickname given to the man who, at a moment's notice, would pick up an elderly woman in his car and drive her to the doctor's office for free. He was a gentle, easy-going person, liked by everyone. Through his heartfelt kindness he set an example for the people of Lemforde and he was respected in the community. He had been a medic on a mine sweeper in World War I and volunteered as a fireman in the village. But it was his sense of community and harmony that endeared him to everyone.

Many years later, after I grew into adulthood and had a family of my own, I began to deeply miss my father. I realized that I never really had a papa who took me for a walk holding my hand or gave me a piggyback ride. I never knew the joy of making him proud at a performance or recital. Even now, I feel a void, a need to recall even the most vague memories I had of the past. But most of all I feel pain, that it was the Nazis who took all that from me — and did the same to countless other families.

I woke up one morning at the age of 45 and I was crying. I had awakened from a dream so vivid, so real, so sad, that my tears would not stop. I was crying for my lost father, and for all the lost fathers and mothers and sisters and brothers. In my dream I was still a little girl walking at the edge of a dense forest on the outskirts of Schermbeck where I was living with my grandparents. It was early morning and the sun was hovering on the horizon, the mist draping everything in pale pink glow. Spotted toadstools and blueberry bushes were the playground for chipmunks and rabbits that dashed about in the rustle of leaves.

Oddly, amongst all the beauty I feel anxious and begin to run until I am almost out of breath. I stop and, looking straight ahead, see my father standing in the distance. Filtered sunbeams cast an eerie light where he stands and he appears to see me. He looks so alive, so neat and well-dressed. "My papa!" I shout and run toward him. Can I really put my arms around him? Can I again feel his kiss on my forehead? I fight for breath only to be able to reach him. I stumble but am getting closer. I am almost there, when I lift my eyes and see that he is gone. Vanished.

It was then that I had awakened, my heart heavy once

again with his loss. How strange it seemed to me in retrospect, how ironic, that in my four years alive with my father we never set foot in the village of Schermbeck together.

I've had the same dream three times, yet never again after I returned to Schermbeck and looked for that forest. It was gone, too. Unfortunately, most of what remains from the dreams of my youth was destroyed in the nightmare years during the Holocaust.

Our family (left to right): Henny Leser, Hulda Zadek, Bertha Kann, Opa Adelsheimer, Louis Silbermann, Hanna Silbermann; Lisel Leser in front

3 | OPA

"Ein Gedenkbuch" published in Berlin in 1932 is dedicated to the 12,000 Jewish soldiers who shed their blood for the Fatherland in the first World War. Even President Von Hindenburg, then leader of Germany, acknowledged receipt of the book, noting that he accepted it in honorable memory of those Jews who had died in the line of duty fighting for their country.

With all of this heroism part of their so-recent past, most German Jewish men felt that they had played an important role in the war. True, they had lost, but they had indeed fought for Germany and survived to help rebuild it. So it was with my father and also Uncle Ziegfried in Berlin, who was decorated with the Iron Cross, the medal of honor. But, as with everything else, all of that changed in 1933 with the rise of Adolf Hitler to power. It wasn't long before he proclaimed himself *Fuhrer und Riechskanzler* (Leader and Reich Chancellor) and by law gained the full support of the military for his Final Solution and deadly march into the pages of history.

For our family and many Jews, it was still life as usual. My father had four brothers and a sister and my mother had three sisters and a brother, so we traveled by train from Berlin to Schermbeck on the Rhine, to Lemfoerde in Lower Saxony, and to the Saarbasin in the south on many joyous occasions. There were births and birthdays to celebrate and Chanuka for gift giving. Summers were spent in the country and there, in Schermbeck, the cousins spent weeks helping grandpa Opa in the garden, playing at the lake, feeding the ducks and swans, and visiting the gristmill to watch the grain ground into flour for the local farmers.

Soon the Nuremberg Laws restricted our travel unless special permission was granted. Before I knew what was happening, my father was dead and I was living in my grandparents' house. The town was different, the surroundings were different. I didn't know the neighbors and doubted if I would ever feel comfortable there. I wondered, too, whether I would ever get used to the strange bedroom into which I'd been moved.

But Schermbeck proved to be such a beautiful village, and it still is. The old windmill by the lake, the pungent fragrance of water lilies, the reeds and wildflowers, the black and white swans on the still waters. These were the feelings when I first came to Schermbeck, which is near the Dutch border. My Opa and Oma and Aunt Paula were not strangers to me for we had visited often, and I knew that they loved me and would care for me. Although I missed my mother with an ache that was always with me, I soon forgot my old neighborhood in Lemfoerde, as children do, and became absorbed in my new life.

Unfortunately, when I arrived my grandmother was ill in a way that was hard for me to understand, drifting in and out between past and present. So it was my grandfather, my beloved Opa, who was the center around which my world turned. Stocky and broad-shouldered, a bit stooped with age but always gentle and kind with me, he was my source of security in a world that had so recently turned upside-down.

Many times Opa would take my hand, shut the door behind us, and walk with me down the main street, past the blacksmith shop and town hall and across the little bridge that spanned the creek. I always had to stop there because I loved the sound of the water splashing against the rocks. Opa would let me pick some little white berries that looked like beads and would patiently wait while

Grandfather Opa, born in Lemforde 1865 and perished at Theresienstadt 1943

I laid them on the ground and stomped on them with my feet until they popped.

I had a sandbox that Opa built for me in the garden at the end of the path beside the red-roofed gazebo. When things turned bad in Germany, this was where we went to escape, to feel safe. Inside the gazebo there were garden tools, a round table, and two iron chairs. After working in the garden we would go there and eat sandwiches with cheese from Holland and homemade bread, and Opa would enjoy his coffee. Even though were toiling in the thick, musty dirt, Opa always was properly dressed in his shirt and vest and watchfob, for he was a dignified man who believed that certain kinds of behavior were proper.

And so my childhood went, harvesting the garden with Opa, sharing meals and celebrating Jewish holidays with our family, and playing, unencumbered with the portent of events that signaled the end of "the good times."

In 1935 all Jews lost their citizenship. I was no longer allowed to attend school and Opa was not permitted to continue his modest cattle business. Local butchers who used to buy from him were told to buy from someone else. Suddenly, he was no longer welcome in the Kegelclub. The other members, the dentist, the druggist, the tavern owner and other businessmen, men he thought his friends, no longer sought his company.

There were ominous signs of coming disaster, humiliating and depressing. I was small but I knew it was no longer safe for Jews in Germany. And my worst fears came true the day Opa gathered us around and said, "It is time to leave. We are not wanted here any longer."

Yet, when I return to Schermbeck now I can still remember the good times — walking down the main street, crossing the bridge, picking the little white berries. Unfortunately, gone are the synagogue, the garden gate which used to squeak when Opa pushed it aside, and the gazebo, my safe haven. But the taste of the fruits is still on my tongue, and the joy of having shared those moments in my paradise will surely never leave me. Gone are the things. Gone are the places. Gone are the people. But not the memories.

4 | DEATH OF A QUEEN

One person who I shall never forget, whose strength and goodwill shaped the person I am today, is my Aunt Paula Adelsheimer. Her short life bounded by two extremes: one day, queen of her home town, an object of respect and admiration; a decade later, deported and gassed to death at Birkenau. I still ask myself how this could have happened to such as giving, loving person. Yet, hers is a story worth telling.

Paula was the youngest child of Gustav and Emma Adelsheimer (my mother's parents) and grew up in their home on Mittel Strasse. When I came to Schermbeck and was taken in as part of the family, she responded to my loneliness and cared for me as she would her own child. Unfortunately, she would never experience having a child for herself.

At the time that Paula was growing up and until 1926 the synagogue in Schermbeck buzzed with activity, especially during the Jewish holidays, festivals and celebrations throughout the year. The 90 Jews of the town were well accepted and lived a pleasant life alongside approximately 1,000 Christians. Young boys were taught Hebrew by teachers who prepared them for their bar mitzvah. By the time I arrived, there were

Aunt Paula, "Queen of the Scheutzenfest," born in 1906 and murdered in Auschwitz in 1943

no longer enough Jews to support the synagogue and it sat empty and deserted. I remember that it seemed so sad to me to see weeds growing through the floor as I stood on tiptoes and peered through the dusty window glass.

In 1929 Paula was a charming 24-year-old at the prime of her life. She was of medium height, small boned and delicate, and wore her hair in soft curls around her face. She was quiet, modest, and well-spoken as befit the daughter of a successful businessman and respected member of the community. She enjoyed her lifestyle and various Christian friends who often accompanied her on trips into the countryside for picnics and bicycle rides.

The days in Schermbeck were highlighted with parades, festivals, and fairs that drew people from surrounding towns and villages. One such occasion was the Kilian Scheutzenfest, a yearly, non-militaristic event that was universally celebrated throughout this part of Germany. It lasted for days and there was food, a parade, and shooting competitions. A huge tent was erected, called a Bier Halle, and the townspeople all turned out for the different competitions.

The Scheutzenfest, as the name implies, was centered on how well the local men could shoot. The highlight of the event was a contest to see whether the marksmen, many of whom had served in Germany's army during World War I, could shoot down a wooden bird mounted high in a tree. Many men participated in turn, and the one who shot down the last part of the bird was crowned the king. He then chose a queen, someone who would serve for the entire year. In 1929, at a time when all was well with Germany, when Jews and Christians shared food and drinks and laughter, a Jewish queen was chosen, a Jewish queen named Paula. It had never happened before, and she thought it an honor to represent her village.

At her coronation the mayor, in top hat and tails, along with his wife, shared the white horse-drawn carriage with the king and queen. I can just imagine my Opa standing in the doorway of our house as the parade passed by with his daughter on display, her tiara sparkling in the sunlight, queen of the Scheutzenfest.

But as with almost every fond remembrance from that time there is another story to tell, an often sad and grim story. And so it was for my Aunt Paula.

In 1933 there was a new burgermeister in Schermbeck and a new party to rule all of Germany, for a man named Adolf Hitler was in command. The years of friendship and security for Jews were over and Aunt Paula's celebrity status was no more. No more accolades and honors. No more parades. In fact, where she once could mingle and share her joy with others, she must now be inconspicuous.

Depressed and lonely, she quietly took care of her home and her parents — and me. My grandmother was ill and as a dutiful daughter Paula stayed home and ran the household. She seemed to be in good spirits at the time of my arrival, but like the rest of us that would be short-lived.

When we later fled to Berlin and went into hiding she lived in a small, dark room with her mother and father, seeing daylight only as she came and went to work. In 1940, frail as she was, she was conscripted by an electrical manufacturer to do forced labor. I lost touch with her when we made it to America. Letters of desperation found us in 1941. The urgency to escape was overwhelming, but there was nowhere to go and no way to get out. The gates had closed.

I learned that in 1942 Aunt Paula and all of our family who could not get out were deported to Warsaw. From there, Paula, the once radiant queen of Schermbeck, whose future sparkled as brightly as her tiara, was sent to Birkenau where she died. It was an unfitting end for such a vibrant person, a woman who personified the Jewish spirit and zest for living, a human being who deserved better.

I honor Aunt Paula's memory each Yom Hashoa. The tablecloth she made for my mother is now in my possession and each year I place it on the table on the Bima (altar). On it rest the six memorial candles and, as I light each one, she is with me again, and I remember.

5 | KRISTALLNACHT

As conditions for Jews deteriorated, more and more people in Germany and Austria, where the Anschluss meant that all anti-Semitic decrees now applied there as well, felt the urgency to leave. But where would we go?

The Evian Conference in France sought to alleviate immigration bottlenecks to other countries, but 32 attending nations failed to change their quotas to allow more immigrants into their lands. Some nations, such as Switzerland, even took measures to restrict Jews from immigrating by asking German officials to mark a "J" on all Jewish passports. Even the United States, "land of the free," was slow in offering sanctuary.

Instead, for many Jews, the answer was made for them. The Nazis would round people up like cattle and force them to move by train or on foot to ghettos and concentration camps. There, the people who only days before experienced the freedoms and goodwill of their towns and villages, were subjected to starvation, disease and torture. They often had to learn new languages, other customs, and try to survive within the barbed-wire walls of their Nazi home.

Some Jews tried to go into hiding or join partisan forces in the woods.

At home on the main street — Mittel Strasse — of Schermbeck

Others, many children, tried to pass themselves as non-Jews, creating new identities and denying their family heritage in exchange for freedom. For us, the decision was made to begin the emigration process immediately. Though we had affidavits from America and a family to guarantee our welfare, we had to wait for a quota number from Stuttgart, and they were at a minimum.

In 1938, my Uncle Arthur, my mother's brother, his wife and son Harry left Germany and emigrated to the United States. Two years later, my Aunt Bertha, Mother's sister, her husband and two sons also left for America. These two events were difficult to fathom for the family members left behind. Each of us was torn between elation that they had gotten away from this worsening situation and the sadness that we may never see them again. In essence, it was the end of life as we knew it.

For me, I still had some friends from school, but the

Nuremberg Laws prohibited me from continuing an education I had barely begun. My beloved twin cousins in Berlin were also forced to give up their education. There were now restrictions on age levels of those who could leave. My Aunt Hulda, their mother, wrote from Berlin, "We must do something quickly. The girls will be 19 soon." I was young, but I already knew that when a person became an adult, their life was expendable. I didn't want to think about what that meant for my dear cousins.

Being one of only a few Jewish children in the village made it easy for Nazi authorities to make sure that no German child played with me. It was a time in Germany when everyone was watched and they, in turn, watched one another. Many people were upset and angry about how they were being treated, but Hitler's trap had been sprung. Those who had pledged allegiance to his tyranny in return for food, clothing, and other necessities now found themselves at war with their consciences.

On the nights of November 9 and 10, 1938, throughout Germany and Austria an anti-Jewish outrage was committed. History shows it was provoked by the assassination of Ernst von Roth, secretary of the German embassy in Paris, who was shot by Hershel Grynszpan, the son of Polish-Jewish parents living in Germany until their deportation early in 1938. When the diplomat died, measures of retaliation followed. There were widespread attacks on Jews, Jewish property and synagogues, climaxing five years of anti-Semitic measures under Hitler's rule. The SA, SS and Gestapo were successful in burning or destroying 267 synagogues. Many Jews were killed and more than 30,000 Jewish men and boys were sent to Dachau, Buchenwald and Sachsenhausen.

Half a century later in 1988 the German government announced via proclamation that this night, known as Kristallnacht, would be given a new name, Reichpogromnacht, the night of terror, destruction and murder. For me, it will always be Kristallnact, "the night of breaking glass."

It was twilight on November 9, 1938 when I kissed my grandparents goodnight and followed Aunt Paula up the winding stairway to my room. She tucked me into my feather-stuffed bed and I fell sound asleep, the smell of my Opa's cigar a silent signal that all was well. Suddenly, at around 10 o'clock, I was awakened by a sound that frightened me so that my teeth began to chatter. I ran to the window and saw boys and men in brown uniforms carrying bricks and torches as they marched through the street. They were singing awful songs about Jews and, even at my young age, I knew they were going to do something very bad.

I hurried to join my family, who were huddled in my grandmother's tiny, dark bedroom in the middle of the house, as the shouts and epithets grew louder. We cried and screamed and did not know if we would survive the night. Then the Nazis burst into our room, telling us to leave the house and that they would burn it to the ground. I remember running from our home accompanied by angry shouts and shattering glass as the village people could only watch in horror. We ran in terror to the only shelter we could find, the Catholic hospital at the end of town. There, the nuns provided us with a haven until the Nazis found us again and we were forced to leave. All of us, together with four other Jewish families, hid in the woods until dawn.

In the morning light, exhausted and in shock, we approached our once-beautiful homes. Most of our belongings lay in the street, broken to pieces. There was not even a chair left for my grandmother to sit on. The Nazis had destroyed everything our family had worked for all these years. Even Opa's cherished yellow canary was trampled to death.

Some of the other townspeople had gone to the aid of their Jewish neighbors and were punished for it as well. Our next-door neighbor, a farmer, tried to help. Within minutes all of the windows in his home were broken. Some neighbors tried to help a Jewish woman who used to clean the synagogue before it was closed. They were beaten for "interfering."

Several hours after dawn some of my school friends came near our house, bewildered by what they saw. Edith, my best friend, stood there the longest, touching her long braids as I looked at her through the broken window, her blonde hair, blue eyes and tiny smile a contrast to my dingy clothes and skin. We were only children and really couldn't understand. Yet neither could the adults. I wanted so much to go with my friend to the lake and play and wash our doll clothes like we used to. But we didn't dare. Her parents had already been called into the burgermeister's office and told to forbid their daughter to play with Jews.

My mother, who had been held at gunpoint with all the other Jews in the abandoned orphanage at Dinslaken, came as soon as she could. She told us how for days she lay in the straw, worried sick and not knowing where or how her children and family were. The Nazis had loaded all of the orphans, over fifty of them, into an empty hay wagon — those who did not fit were made to pull the wagon to the railroad station where they were deported and never heard from again. It was not like the prewar Kindertransport, where thousands of Jewish children were allowed to leave Nazi-occupied countries for refuge. My mother could only imagine what we were going through.

But by joining us my mother provided strength and hope. She hid her tears and never cried in front of us. I had not realized how much I loved her and needed her with me — in fact, how much the whole family needed her. Even when we heard from my sister, Hilda, about the family she lived with, how the shop they owned was destroyed and Hilda escaped by hiding in a closet on the third floor, Mother didn't flinch.

We realized we had survived Kristallnacht, but at great cost to our souls. What we were left with after the brutal events of that second week in November were shattered dreams and tattered curtains, which flapped lifelessly in the broken windows of our once happy home. Hitler's plan had worked; he had broken our spirit. But not our will to live. We realized even in such trying times that our life there was fading. Quietly we had made our plans: We would go to Berlin where I had an aunt and uncle and cousins.

It was December, bitter and cold. While preparing for our journey we had to live with broken windows and without heat during those blustery, gray days. Even the lake had frozen over. But, like a warm ray of sunshine, my brother Herbert appeared. We were glad to see him alive and well, and he provided us with a sense of security, even though he had to hide out in the loft. He set to boarding up the windows and fixing things that had been broken, but our time together was short-lived. The Gestapo came one day and stormed through the house. Herbert hid quietly in the loft, but they found him anyway and forced him into the street. One of the last images I have from that time was my Aunt Paula tossing Herbert a pair of wool socks as they led him away, his final destination Dachau. My other brother Manfred also came back to Schermbeck after Kristallnacht, but my only memory of him is being cradled on his lap at Opa's house. Shortly after his arrival he too was arrested and taken to Buchenwald, where he was beaten and tortured. After several months he was released and, with luck, made his way to England.

Several weeks later, we packed our suitcases and walked away from Schermbeck, our home, for the last time. Dusk was upon us as we stood in the cobblestone street, the rising moon casting faint shadows as we huddled together in front of our once-vibrant home, a home that had known generations of our family. As we were leaving, Opa gave his pocket knife to the neighbor's son next door. It was then that I saw my good friend, Irmgard, leaning out her second-story window. She was a Christian who lived next door along with her three sisters and brother. Through my tears it was difficult to see her short blonde hair, blue eyes and tiny smile. "Where are you going?" she called softly. "I'm not sure," I replied. "I think we're going to a big city to stay with my aunt." "But when will you be back?" she said. I couldn't answer; I did not know. I remembered the winters and summers we had played together in the yard behind our houses. She had been a loyal and sweet friend to me. Impulsively, I tossed my sewing basket to her. She caught it and began to cry.

I took one last glance at my home as we left town that cold day in January of 1939, not knowing whether I would ever come back or even if there would by anything to come back to. As night crept upon the village, we silently walked toward the train station, sneaking away like thieves, I thought. I had made the walk to the station many times, but it never seemed as long as that night. I was glad my mother was there to hold my hand.

As we approached the train station, we knew that we were taking leave of an era. We now knew that this was the beginning of the end. We no longer had the luxury of believing that somehow Hitler would not be able to carry out his plan, that all of this temporary insanity would disappear. I can still see my Opa, proud, his head covered with a prayer shawl, reaching his hands toward the heavens and asking "Why?"

I ask myself that question to this day. The Enabling Act of 1934 allowed unjustified arrests, beatings and torture all in the name of Der Fuhrer. The people who marched into our town that night, singing their hate songs, came from a neighboring town. I later discovered that the Nazis from Schermbeck went to a nearby village to conduct their own terrorism. Was it easier for them to hurt and humiliate people they did not know? Were strangers less human than people from one's own town? I cannot make much sense from those two nights in November, 1938 — but that can be said for many nights throughout Hitler's reign of terror.

The Reichstag (or democratic republic) had been abolished, boycotts called for, and concentration camps built all under the guise that Hitler would make Germany once again a wonderful place to live, that is, unless you were Jewish. In 1930 there were half a million Jews in Germany. By 1938 nearly one-third had been forced to leave — and they may have been the fortunate ones.

24

6 | ESCAPE

We arrived in Berlin in the winter of 1939. There we found cold and snow and very little food available on our ration card, which I remember clearly because of the large red "J" on it (standing for Jew) and the many coupons cut out. There was no meat to be had for Jews and only horse meat or mutton for the lucky Berliners who could afford it. Mostly we ate potatoes and vegetables and a dish called *eintopf*, which by law had to be cooked once a week. It consisted of whatever leftovers could be found as well as potatoes. We always made eintopf on Thursday. I remember that the secret police, the SA, could enter any home and actually lift the lid to see what we were cooking.

My grandparents and Aunt Paula had a dark and dreary apartment on the second floor of a private home. Mother and I moved in with her sister, Hulda, and her husband Sigfried, as well as my twin cousins, Ruth and Hanna. By all accounts we were lucky: I had my mother and she had me, and we had the comfort of family and their love to help us through the next two years in Berlin, years that comprised dangerous days and sleepless nights.

During that time Nazi Germany was able to invade and occupy Czechoslovakia, Poland, Denmark, Norway, Nether-

The author as a youngster in
Koerner Park, Berlin

lands, Belgium, Luxembourg and France. The first Jewish ghetto, an area walled in barbed wire, was constructed in Poland. Many other Jews were refused admittance and lived in deplorable conditions in the frontier town of Zbaszyn. The Nazis controlled the media and there was no way we could know what had transpired.

So we lived out our days in a quiet, residential part of Berlin near Koerner Park, waiting for our break that would mean freedom in America. I spent much of my time enjoying the park, its ivy-covered walls directly across the street, the backdrop for vivid flowers that changed with each season. An ornate fountain sat at the center of the park, neatly trimmed bushes and paths encircling it. It was everything beautiful that Germany was not.

Missing the familiar pastoral setting and green of Schermbeck, I would ask Hanna and Ruth to take me to the park. There, the twins would take turns reading wonderful stories and walking me along verdant paths as I pushed the doll buggy that once belonged to them. Sometimes, when I was old enough, they would wave good-bye and go off with their friends for awhile. I would sit on the white wooden bench and rock my doll in the buggy. I could hear the splashing water from the fountain and smell the fragrant flowers and I felt secure.

One day a sign was posted on the gate to the park, a sign that read *"Juden Verboten,"* "No Jews." It meant I could no

26

longer enter my favorite place. I could no longer take my doll for walks. No more fountain. No flowers. It was all taken away from me, the way my home had been taken away at Schermbeck. The Nazis once again were in control, their huge anti-aircraft guns littering the green lawns, turrets aimed at the sky in startling contrast to the beauty of the fountain. It wasn't a safe place for my doll; in fact, no place was safe.

There was little to do once the schools were shut down and Jewish university students like Hanna and Ruth, as well as Jewish professors, were expelled. We spent our days knitting and crocheting or cooking what little food we had. The Nazis had effectively cut the Jews off from their educational, cultural and social roots. For now we would have to live indoors with the blinds drawn, seeking whatever comfort we could from each other and praying to get out of the hell that was Berlin. I never felt safe. I remember wearing a coat with a hood which I would pull over my face whenever I was on the street or in a shop. I never looked anyone in the eyes; never greeted a stranger.

The war was now in full fury, and it was taking its toll on Germany. By 1940 disease was widespread in Berlin, and I contracted both diphtheria and scarlet fever. Each time I was quarantined in one of the Quonset huts that were part of the hospital complex. When mother came to visit me she was only permitted to stand outside a tiny window and wave. I recall that we exchanged glances and made funny faces and that I cried when she left. It was very difficult for her to leave, too, because air raids came every night.

When I finally recovered and returned home, it seemed that we spent most of our time in the basement food locker which doubled as a bomb shelter. The sirens were so loud and frightening that we almost fell over each other in an attempt to get down the stairs. My cousins, who had already learned to speak English, would try to teach me songs to distract me.

In May of 1941 we received word that our immigration papers were in order and a quota number was available. Abruptly and with no further warning, we were told to leave the next morning. But to leave meant moving on with no money, few belongings, and little else. Some people chose to emigrate to other European countries, the United States, Palestine and Australia, but the flood of refugees created delays and disappointments of not being allowed entry.

Our other choice, a choice that more than 200,000 Jews were faced with, was staying put, hiding out, and praying to Almighty God that Hitler and his henchmen would be overthrown. Many people did not want to leave their homes. Some even had pride for their country, as out of control as it was. Most had no choice but to stay.

We packed a bag: fifty pounds of clothing, my precious doll, Puppchen, and Mutti's wedding ring were all we took. We said farewell to our family members who had to stay behind and believed that everyone would soon follow. So it was with optimism that we boarded the ship for the Americas, but like many of our fellow passengers riding the wave of freedom and escape, we would come to learn that most of our relatives, who had done so much for us and wished us well upon our release, were destined to perish.

In the years to follow, 1.1 million Jews were executed at Auschwitz, and another 1.5 million at Sobibor, Belzec and Treblinka. My mother's parents and sister, my aunts, my uncle, my cousins and grandparents would never be heard from again. When I left Germany that day almost sixty years ago, I

had no idea that my ties with the past, my lineage, would be crushed under the boot of Nazi oppression like the tiny white berries on the sidewalk of my youth.

Postcard of the "Mousinho" as it sets sail from Lisbon to New York, June 21, 1941

But my mother once again found the strength to help us pick up the pieces. Once safe in Lisbon, she made sure I had a beautiful new pair of blue woven leather shoes with red laces. She also made sure Hilda and I ate well and that we caught up on our sleep. And most of all, she assured us that being seasick was a small price to pay for the freedom that came at the end of the long voyage across the Atlantic Ocean.

Weeks later, as we pulled into New York harbor and were greeted by the Statue of Liberty, I realized that we were in America and that our prayers had been answered. My mother would be reunited with her brother and sister who had left Germany two years before, and we could begin our lives anew. Immediately after debarking, my Uncle Nathan and cousin Kurt picked us up in a Chevy with a rumble seat. We drove directly to Pittsburgh, Pennsylvania where the rest of our family was waiting. It was good to see them all again.

My mother decided that we would be best served if I went to a foster home so that she could go to work as a housekeeper. Although I wouldn't be with my Mutti all of the time, at least we were safe. It was August 1941 and school would soon start. I was afraid. Everything was so new, the language, the people. And the city was so big. I was living in a little room with a German-speaking family, but I began to miss my mother. She worked all day and was going to school to learn English and when she came to visit me at Aunt Bertha's on her day off, we would practice a few words and laugh.

It took two years for my mother and Hilda to save enough to rent a third-floor apartment. We had a living room where we all slept on sleeper sofas, a kitchen, bath, and in the hall was an icebox. How happy I was to be with my family, my Mutti, again. After months of serving strangers she now could cook and clean for herself and her children. Mother still worked as a domestic and I began to earn money baby-sitting. We worked hard at making a new life, but we were thankful to be gone from that place. I even found time to enjoy comic books. It was a long way from the menacing shouts, air raid sirens, and bombings that had become synonymous with living in Germany. Happy as we were, we couldn't help but wonder what fate held for our family who remained there.

Over the years in Pittsburgh, Jews from Germany and Austria formed the Friendship Club and, during the High Holidays we held our own services according to German tradition. Originally we organized to help one another as needed, but that quickly grew into casual get-togethers every Saturday night to play cards and socialize. I can remember making potato salad and wieners with my mother and serving coffee and macaroon cake for dessert. How strange it was that just a few years ago our life could be so fraught with turmoil and now we were having tasty meals in the quiet comfort of our own home.

Many Jews experienced the luxury of escape during those difficult times, yet I wonder how many feel regret, even guilt, for those left behind. What allowed us to come to this plentiful country which seemed so tolerant of our beliefs? Why were we able to leave while others in our family, on our block, in our neighborhood were left behind to suffer and die? It is a question that I wrestle with almost every day.

But soon the war was over and our thoughts turned to the easy living of these United States. The soldiers returned home heroes and were greeted with ticker-tape parades and great fanfare. An economic boom from the war allowed everyone to improve their lot in life. By now most people had refrigerators, but we still had an icebox. I felt sorry for the man who used to lug our 25-pound block of ice all the way up to our third floor. On my way home from school one day in 1947, I saw a truck unloading refrigerators. I ran into the store and gave the proprietor my wristwatch as a down payment and then ran home with much excitement to tell Mother of my find. We got our money together and the following day we were the proud owners of a Kelvinator: We were Americans.

But things weren't so easy for countless other Jews who had survived the Holocaust and war only to be left with nothing but the blemish of being branded a Jew. For many, their entire families were wiped out and they did not want to live in Germany or Europe for that matter. They had no homes or businesses to return to, and there were still reports that Jews were being persecuted, particularly in Eastern Europe where the Communists were in control.

Until they could decide where to go and what to do, many Jews stayed in Displaced Persons (D.P.) camps, which had been set up by the United Nations Relief Agency (UNRA) and the Red Cross. There they would receive food, clothing, medical assistance and respite from the trials of war. The camps also offered assistance in searching for family members. Social workers helped people get their paperwork in order to immigrate to countries such as the United States, England, Australia and Palestine, but it wasn't easy. Palestine was under British occupation, so there was no Jewish homeland yet. In fact, not until 1948 when Israel was recognized as a state by the United Nations would Jews have a home. It was that same year that the U.S. passed the Displaced Persons Act which allowed 400,000 refugees, both Jewish and non-Jewish victims of the war, to enter the country over a period of years. But, for many, it was too late.

Years later, after my sister, brother and I had married and moved on, Mother rented an efficiency apartment within walking distance of a senior citizen center where she felt at home doing volunteer work. When she wasn't carrying armfuls of sheets or preparing cancer dressings, she was off to the bakery to get bagels for the special club breakfast every Thursday. It was one of many little things she did that made life special for others. It wasn't until years later, after her death, that I realized just how willing she was to help. The most moving words came from the janitor of the senior citizen center, who said that before the special breakfast every Thursday, Mother would bring him a coffee and bagel and wish him a good day.

7 | THE SEWING BASKET

Back in Europe, people were sorting out their lives, salvaging what had escaped the wrath of Hitler and the bombings that ended his reign. In Schermbeck, my friend Irmgard had survived the nightly air raids, the deprivation and hunger that had become part of everyday living. She also withstood the economic and spiritual strain as Germany collapsed at the hands of the allied forces. Through it all she had kept a wooden suitcase built for ease of escape and to withstand the battering it took as she scurried to and from the bunker during air raids. It was the only thing that remained from her life before the rise and fall of the Third Reich.

After the war, Irmgard married and had a family. From the films, books, and records that appeared after 1945 telling about the murder of millions of Jews in concentration camps, my good friend was convinced that I was never coming back. She prayed it wasn't so, but she was sure that I had been a victim.

I had for a long time blocked the tragic past from my memory. Like the belongings and favorite things from my youth, my thoughts had been all but erased from my life. But in 1981, when Reverend Bornebusch made contact with me,

A piece of the past reclaimed in 1983

a new life began for me — a life of memories. I began to recall events, people, and places that I had suppressed because they were either too painful or hurtful to remember.

The Reverend encouraged me to return to Schermbeck, a thought that frightened me as if the Kristallnacht were upon us again. What would I see? How would I feel? Was it something I wanted to do? Fragmented ideas and notions shattered my concentration. A wave of anxiety made me numb. After a pause, I said that I would do it.

News of my return was published in a local German newspaper and, as luck would have it, Irmgard saw my picture. She no longer lived in our village, but she was so overwhelmed that she decided to write to me: "Dear Marga. Now that I know you are alive and well, I am so very happy. I would very much like to see you again. Please let me know. There is so much I have to share with you."

I received her letter and, tears running down my face, I decided that returning to Schermbeck was the right thing to do. It would be more than a trip down memory lane; I would be getting my life back. The village, the church bells so crystal clear with few noises to interfere. The lake, where ducks and swans honked in symphony with the croaking frogs. Oh how I remembered my Schermbeck. The clickety-clack of horse hooves on the cobblestone streets, pots and pans clanking from behind the doors of each house. And what of my grandfather's garden? The squeaky gate? The gazebo?

I have returned to Schermbeck on several occasions, but

there will always be a fondness for that reunion with Irmgard. We embraced and shared tears and fears from our past, of Kristallnacht and the day I left. It was as if we were those two little girls again, enjoying each other's company during a peaceful time in Germany. Then, without a word, Irmgard walked to her dining room china closet and retrieved a curious pouch. When she placed it in my hands I grew dizzy with joy. It was my sewing basket! She had kept it safe, among her finest china and religious artifacts, hoping that one day I might return for it.

She explained that she had hidden the sewing basket in the wooden suitcase her father had made during the war, keeping it safe from wear and tear. Years later, when her children asked if they could play with it, the answer was always no. But when they were old enough to understand, she told them the story of a little Jewish girl who lived next door when she was a child. She told them how we had played together and that it was a keepsake from a very good friend who was made to leave her home one night because of the Nazi persecution of Jews. The sewing basket had weathered the storm of war and, now, as it had for decades, symbolized our lifelong friendship that had endured so much.

But there was so much else I needed to retrieve from my past. The sewing basket was a bittersweet reminder of all I had once — and all I had lost.

8 | RECLAIMING MY PAST

One day in 1970 Aunt Bertha gave me back my past. It was so simple; she did it with a box of pictures. Dog-eared, old Kodachromes the color of coffee showed people dressed in clothing from half a century ago. In my hands I held moments of my life frozen in time. People and faces, places that brought such longing, pain and tears. I spent that autumn day looking at photographs of my family, wondering what they might have done in the world had they been permitted to live the rest of their lives. Was it possible that I had lost two entire generations to the evils of war? And how many other Jewish families were suffering the same loss, a gap in lineage and tradition that may never be bridged? As much as I enjoyed seeing long-lost relatives again, I couldn't help but feel remorse and anger that they were taken away from me.

One picture, however, carries a significant sentiment for me: It is of my twin cousins, Hanna and Ruth. How familiar their faces are even to this day. Identical they were, like perfect mirror images. Refined and feminine, on the cusp of womanhood. I often wonder what their lives would have given the world had they been allowed to live. They had talked about practicing medicine, and I can almost see them in white lab coats, taking turns looking into a microscope. What might they have discovered? How many lives could they have saved? Oh, how I missed them. Memories of my times with them flood my mind. How they let me play with their friends. The baby buggy they gave me for my doll. The times they sang songs to make me feel better. I remember them sitting on my bed and reading stories to me. And most of all I remember the three of us in Koerner Park.

The twins, Ruth and Hanna Zadek, whose future was tragically cut short by the Nazis

But that was another time, another place. As my life and story unfold, I often catch my breath at the twists and turns that fate has dealt me and, although many terrible things have happened, sometimes I cannot believe my good fortune. That is why I chose to return to Schermbeck and will continue to do so as long as I live.

Over the years I have searched for tangible pieces of my past, something in addition to the sewing basket that might help me reconnect with my long-lost family. Something like Opa's *tfillin* and prayer shawl or our *tzedakah* box where on special occasions we put money for the poor. Where were all the dear things I had treasured and had to leave behind? Had they been tossed carelessly in a pile at Theresienstadt to gather dust and rot? Were they burned during bombings? God forbid, had Nazis pilfered them? I just had to find a touchstone to the past.

On one of my visits to Schermbeck, I decided to return to my birthplace in Lemfoerde. It was then that my prayers were answered. In 1982 I had come back to visit my father's grave and meet with friends of my older sister who still lived in the village. During our conversation someone said that a family living in the village might have our *esstisch*, our dining room table.

I went limp with the prospect of again seeing the oak table that had been the centerpiece of our family's existence. Generations of my family had broken bread and discussed their hopes and dreams around that sturdy piece of wood. There had been great food served on it, beautiful Shabbats, and meaningful seders conducted by my grandparents and father. If I could only lay my hands on its smooth surface once again.

I trembled with excitement as I arrived at Elli's home, the humble house a fitting sanctuary for such a treasured family heirloom. Elli, who seemed more excited than I, welcomed me with a hug. Without delay, she ushered me into the kitchen and removed the tablecloth. Sure enough, it was our table, solid oak with a split down the middle. Feeling weak-kneed, I sat and rubbed its worn surface, reminiscing about the good times and laughter and, yes, sometimes discipline that was shared around this monolith to our family. I could almost envision Mutti serving dinner, father quietly sitting by.

The memories, the family, were still alive in that work of wood. It had survived all that the Nazis could throw at it, the long split symbolizing the Nazis' attempt to separate our kin. But there it stood, strong and sturdy like our family, worn but not destroyed, old but not forgotten.

I shared a glass of wine with Elli and resisted the emo-

tional draw to put my face against its worn surface and cry for all the wasted years, all the lost lives.

While I struggled with the overwhelming memories that came with my good fortune, Elli began to tell the story of our table. For years it had stood in the kitchen of a farm house in Lower Saxony where the Broi family sat comfortably for each meal. No one ever questioned why this table matched nothing else in the entire household, why its ugly mustard brown finish was never repainted. But Elli knew. She knew that the table was the only thing left from a whole set of furniture from the Silbermann home. It was a special table, her mother had told her. It belonged to her best friend, Hanna Silbermann, a Jewish neighbor. She recounted how her mother told of the family and how Hanna's husband, my father, had been a hero in World War I, but had died when the Gestapo came to arrest him in 1934.

Elli explained that when our family had to split up and leave Lemfoerde her mother was given the dining room set for which my mother had no use. She promised Mutti that she would take good care of it and always remember where it came from — and that she did for many years.

In fact, at the age of 93, after years of loving care, Elli's mother gave the table, all that was left of the original set, to her. She explained correctly that it was three generations old and that not only did the Silbermann family raise their children at this table, but so had their father's father before them.

I later learned that the table was so old and full of splinters that one day my uncle put his brush to it and what should have looked like oak came out mustard and brown that still coated the ageless table before me. I couldn't stop staring at the simple piece of furniture. I was trying to concentrate on Elli's story and take it all in without missing a thing. I sipped more wine and asked her to continue.

Elli recounted that her mother never so much as put a nail into the table and would never think of painting it. She wanted to preserve it just the way she received it. Elli said her mother realized that most of our family was probably killed by the Nazis, but that there could be a survivor, in which case the table could be returned to them. One of her last requests was that if any of the Silbermanns ever returned to Lemfoerde that the table be given to them.

I was stunned by the respect this gentile family showed for our cherished table and our past. I was even more taken aback when Elli insisted I accept the table as her mother had wished. In silence, wiping away tears of joy and sorrow, I nodded yes. I would take my past back home.

Today, this precious piece of my family's past stands proudly in my home in Pennsylvania. On it are old pictures and a family album, a glove knitted by my Aunt Paula, and a knitted holder from my twin cousins as well as a fork and spoon that they once used. To most people it looks like a wooden table, but for me it represents life, hope, and a testament for the future that we must continue to have faith in humanity. It stands like a monument, a symbol of survival, and a reminder that Hitler did not totally succeed in his quest for the Final Solution.

9 | "YOU ARE MY FIRST CALLER"

One of the people I recall who sat at our table was Aunt Bertha, petite and meticulously groomed, always a smile turning up at the corners of her mouth. Animated, charming, and eager to talk, Bertha, my mother's sister, was the matriarch of our family. She made everyone happy.

Her life filled with excitement and people, Bertha had a unique way of greeting people who telephoned. She would say in slightly accented English, "You are my first caller." How often had I heard this? I think she used this greeting with everyone who called, but I can't be sure. All I know is that was her way of making us feel all right.

Bertha spent her childhood in Schermbeck, too, and she knew it so well that we often had wonderful conversations about "the old times." When we talked about a particularly special moment, her eyes would widen, she'd clap her hands and say, *"Ach das habe ich bald vergessen!"* (Oh! I almost forgot that!). Then we would giggle like little girls.

How I relished talking about my family with someone who had shared their past. We would sit for hours and recall landmarks, special events, and all of the people who had been taken from our lives. One such story began when Bertha was in her middle twenties. She left Schermbeck and married a man from the south of Germany and they had two sons.

My uncle, Bertha's husband, was Nathan Kann, a serious man who had a flourishing scrap business that allowed my aunt to keep a good home. Their two sons were good students and, together, they were a happy family. Happy, that is, until Kristallnacht when 13 Gestapo agents ransacked their home. One Nazi showed some pity and allowed Bertha to hide her son, Jules, in a bedroom where he would not be taken, while my uncle was dragged from the house without a chance even to say good-bye.

For the longest time there was no news of Nathan. We had heard that the men and boys were being taken to concentration camps and we wondered if he would ever return. Fortunately, the elder son Kurt had been studying in Frankfurt and he got away before the Nazis could arrest him. He fled by motorcycle over hills and valleys until the bike literally fell apart. Then, by foot, he hiked until he reached Saarbrucken. Exhausted and wracked with hunger, at least he was safe.

Finally, to everyone's joy, Nathan eventually came home. While there was time, they made plans and secured papers to go to America: They would have to sacrifice everything for a chance at free-

Aunt Bertha Adelsheimer Kann (1893–1990) escaped to the U.S. in 1939

43

dom. In the United States Bertha's family had to begin anew. Nathan had only known the salvage business and it did not prepare him for work in this new country with its foreign language. So he went to school, learned English and set his focus on being self-employed again. During this time Bertha worked as a domestic, washing floors and windows. Eventually Nathan got a job with a steel company and, after saving his money, he then started his own small business. Both sons joined the U.S. Army where Kurt fought with the Allies on German soil and Jules was with the intelligence service in England. After the war, Jules became a doctor and Kurt followed his father's footsteps in the steel industry.

Her recollections rekindled a few of my own. We did not visit often, but I remember once, when we were in Saarbrucken, my uncle took me out into the dark, snowy December night. I was bundled up to keep warm, but he didn't even wear a coat. He was a rugged man, with a hard face and balding, but he held my hand with a tenderness belying a young child. We soon arrived at a busy part of town where people seemed to be happy and festive. There, the heavy aroma of roasted chestnuts filled the air, and to this day whenever I smell burning wood I'm transported back to the chubby vendor wearing a colorful scarf handing me a bag of nuts my uncle had bought.

I enjoyed hearing Bertha's stories about her past, our past. Those were trying years for all of us. We had survived, but there was always the terrible worry of not knowing what had become of those we had to leave behind. To our great sorrow, and to the greater loss of the Jewish people, by 1946 we knew that they all had perished. It was, and still is, impossible for me to believe that innocent people, the elderly and infirm, the young and promising, would be gassed and burned because they were Jewish.

Often Bertha and I would cry together while reminiscing about the years in Germany when we were growing up. "Why do we cry so readily?" I asked her. "Because we were born by the water of our Schermbeck lake," she would reply. "The tears are for the lake."

My Aunt Bertha Adelsheimer Kann lived to be 97 and fulfilled many of her dreams. She was active and vibrant until her last days, devoted to her grandchildren and great-grandchildren. I still have the urge to pick up the phone and call her, hoping to hear her once again say, "You are my first caller." If I could, I would tell her that I have returned to Schermbeck eleven times since 1981 and each trip she is there with me. I want her to know how many people remember her, the beautiful daughter of Gustav and Emma, her picture hanging on their walls. I would tell her how she is remembered for working with over one hundred men in a large business in Wesel. I would boast that her handcraft is on display in the local museum in Schermbeck. And, most important of all, I would proudly report that her memory lives on in the hearts and minds of the people she knew who are still alive in that tiny village by the lake.

10 | MY RETURN TO SCHERMBECK

Upon my very first visit to Schermbeck the summer of 1981, all of the dreaming and longing to return to the place were my life started came to fruition. After forty-five years of wondering, waiting, agonizing over unanswered questions and untold atrocities, I would be able to face my past. I could sort out the missing details and straighten things out in my mind. And I would be able to satisfy the terrible hunger for what might have been.

Prior to leaving the United States, I had wondered whether I could handle going back to a place where I had been treated so unkindly. I wondered whether anyone would remember, or care, that I was one of the Jews who survived. Worse yet, would there be no response? As I boarded the plane I was juggling a heart full of emotions, ranging from anger to sadness. My family had expressed their feelings to me in no uncertain terms: Never, they said, would they set foot on German soil. But I felt differently. I needed to return, even at the risk of pain and sorrow.

So, there I was, enveloped no longer by dreams but reality. I had been nervous when Wolfgang met me at the airport in Dusseldorf, but returning to Schermbeck would be the ulti-

mate test. Where would I begin?
How would I tackle the moment

that took me back to such a dreadful time in my life? I contemplated these and other questions as I finished breakfast at the Bornebusch home. I asked to be excused and chose to revisit the site of my youth alone.

Approaching the outskirts of Schermbeck I was excited but apprehensive. It had been so long since I was last there. Would I recognize the landmarks? Would they still be there? Then, as if in answer to my silent questioning, the Catholic hospital came into view. There was no change in appearance of the place that harbored us that awful night so long ago. We turned the corner and there was the church, and beyond that the village.

The main street stretched out before me, somewhat shorter than I remembered it. There was the tavern where

47

Opa met with friends, the butcher shop where I longingly had looked at the smoked sausages hanging in the window. The *apotheke,* drugstore, reminded me of the diamond-shaped licorice we used to paste on the back of our hands and lick as we walked to school in the morning. It was all coming back — my childhood was mine again.

Alive with joy, I reveled in the recognition of every street, every alley. Even the gardens hadn't changed. People rode by on bicycles with shopping baskets attached above the rear wheel. Young and old, men, women and children filled the streets. They all were oblivious to my newfound fortune. Yet, with undeniable bitterness, I couldn't help but wonder what my life would have been had I grown up here as should have been my birthright.

That morning I walked alone over the little bridge, past the blacksmith shop and down the street until I could see the corner where our home once stood. Lost in time, I stood there dreaming. I walked to where our front steps used to be and was startled to find myself looking into the display window of a store that sold bathroom fixtures. I remembered then that I had been told the house was bombed and razed in May of 1945, just before the end of the war. Still in a daze, I walked inside and found the approximate spot where our living room would have been.

Just then an elderly woman approached me and wanted to know if I needed any help. "I'm afraid it's too late for that," I replied involuntarily. I stared at the floor. "What do you mean?" she inquired. I explained that this was were the Adelsheimer's home had stood so long ago and that I was returning here for the first time. The woman smiled slightly, then, to my surprise, she said that she recalled the name and believed her brother used to play cards with my Uncle Arthur. Her parents had been our neighbors.

I was sure she was shocked to see me, almost as much as I was to hear that her family was once our neighbors. To her it must have seemed as if a ghost were haunting the place, searching for peace that it never found in life. I stood there for a while, trying hard to remember all the things that had been in our living room, and how we all had shared this space together. I left the building with a heavy heart but satisfied that I had found the ground where our family lived.

Several blocks away I spied the familiar old church. Built in 1100 AD, it had support walls at its base that formed perfect hiding places for a little girl. Seeing the bastion which had survived all these years, I was reminded of the times when I would break with our family tradition of eating only kosher food, and hide in a nook of the wall to eat a piece of sausage I had purchased from the butcher. My little sin went undetected all these years and, now, standing here alone, I secretly wished that someone had caught me . . . and more so, that they were here to share the memory.

On I went, between the alley and George Street where our synagogue once stood. Die Schermbecker Synagogue is where the Jews used to meet and worship, the women sitting upstairs, the men below. It was a very small building, well-kept by a woman who lived next door. Her home also contained the *mikva*, the ritual bath, where all the women of Schermbeck learned to knit while their children ate *zucker butter brot*, homemade bread and butter sprinkled with sugar. Unfortunately, her kindness was not enough to save her from deportation and death at Theresienstadt.

Adolph Ridder worked as a cattle driver for Opa in the 1920s

I knocked on the door of a familiar house and a tall man with white hair and piercing blue eyes opened the door. I recognized him as Adolph Ridder, the man who drove cattle to market for Opa. When I introduced myself as the granddaughter of Gustav Adelsheimer, he cried out, "Oh. That I should live long enough to meet you." He welcomed me in and offered me a seat.

We chatted idly for a while, and then, as if sensing that I was in search of some semblance from my past, Adolph began to talk about Kristallnacht. He recounted how the Nazis grew in number in the weeks preceding that horrible night, and how he feared for his family's welfare. In spite of his disdain for Hitler's rules and edicts, he did not dare greet a Jew on the street for fear of reprisals. He hated what it had done to him and his family, forcing them into a lifestyle that went against all their principles, their basic love for mankind.

I sat quietly and tried to understand how it must have been for those who were not persecuted as Jews yet had to live under the choking yoke of Nazi rule. I wondered if they felt guilt and pain for being helpless in a time of crisis, and for being spared when so many others weren't as lucky. What he said next shed some light on what I'd been thinking.

The man, who suddenly looked much older, said that he had gone to our house the morning after Kristallnacht and

50

hid in the bushes across the street. He watched as my family tried to pick up the pieces of our life from right there in the street. With clarity he recalled my Opa's lament from our ravaged doorway. After all these years, he had not forgotten a thing.

For Adolph the retelling of the whole ordeal was cathartic, a relief he never deliberately sought. For me it was difficult to hear from a witness how the very core of our family's existence was shattered. But I accepted that part of history tied to Schermbeck, Adolph Ridder, and me. It was important to hear from a man who claimed he had no choices because, after all, wasn't that the case for us? Wasn't that the fate of six million Jews who were marched into the gas chambers and murdered? Wasn't that why I needed to come back to Schermbeck?

Years later I visited Adolph and again we talked about Opa, how they were friends, and that night we would never forget. However, it would be the last time we talked about the common denominator of our lives, for he died that night at the age of 96.

The people of today's Schermbeck seem friendly enough. I even met some old classmates, none of whom I remembered, and people who had known my grandparents and my mother. Some had worked for my grandfather when he was still a cattle dealer bringing his herd to market. I met a woman who regularly cleaned house for my family. Each relived a part of the past that was painful for them as well as me. Many expressed shame and guilt for what had happened to my family, but I could only listen and share my stories. In many cases, I came away with a better understanding of what life was like for them in Schermbeck; they, in turn, learned what being a Jew meant to millions of people during the Holocaust.

I walked past the tavern, made a sharp turn and within two minutes I was in the countryside. As I passed through the stone wall that has circled the village since the days of Roman occupation, I was greeted by sights that my eyes hadn't seen in more than forty years. As if by magic, the grist mill, the waterwheel, the pastures and the lake all appeared in front of me. The black and white swans of my memory glided over the calm waters, the ripples from their paddling stretching far into the reeds, cattails and water lilies near the shore. Mallards flew back and forth over the lake, seemingly trumpeting my return, my return to a place where my relatives skated in winter and swam in summer.

It was all coming together now, the fantasy and reality. I still had the longing for everything that was gone, for I knew that what remained were only props surrounded by similar scenery. The houses, the lake, the forest, the sound of church bells, even the hospital were simply tokens of a village I once knew. Schermbeck: The memories are endless. The pungent smell of the blacksmith shop as the hot steel is put to hoof. An aroma of fried potatoes and sauerbraten. Fragrances of boxwood hedges growing everywhere. Being there I still felt my beloved family around me, and I know that this is what remembering is all about. Here I have found my mission: to speak for those who have no voice and no grave. Here in Schermbeck I have given them a place to rest in peace, if only in my heart.

11 | A VALIANT MAN

Much of what I've been able to retrieve from my past in Schermbeck I attribute to my friend Wolfgang Bornebusch, who I think of as my mentor. Wolfgang is a very special, compassionate, honorable, determined and strong man. He is the minister of the Lutheran Church in Schermbeck where I left a piece of my heart, only to retrieve it with the help of this gentle man.

With his deep interest in the Old Testament and Jewish tradition, as well as the history of the Jews in Germany and Europe, Wolfgang decided to involve himself in this knowledge and share it with his community. And so it happened that late in 1970, close to Passover, he was explaining about the seder and how it related to the Christian holiday. Although he thought he was introducing the townspeople to some new learning about how Jews celebrate the Passover-Seder, after the service a woman told him of their Jewish neighbors and how they had shared a matzo with them. Though he knew of the small Jewish cemetery in the center of Schermbeck, he had never thought of it, but in retrospect it seemed quite logical that there had been a Jewish community there.

Slowly he began to question the townspeople about the Jews of Schermbeck, how they lived and what part they played in the community. People were anxious and nervous. They were not ready to discuss the Holocaust. But he was careful to establish a mood of inquiry, free of finger-pointing, looking only for understanding and information. He wanted to inquire how they fit into the community. Some people hesitated. Prior to his questioning, not much discussion came up among the townspeople about the war days and the demise of an authority. Though ashamed, many were able to confide past deeds to a man of the church.

As he learned more, Wolfgang decided to discover what had happened to the Jews of his village. The research was a monumental undertaking in time and effort to say nothing of the emotional drain. Of great assistance was a young student of history, Andrea Kammeier, who researched the archives as far back as 1690. Then came the task of looking for survivors, Jews still alive and willing to cooperate. He wrote several letters and one came to Aunt Bertha who invited him to come to Pittsburgh to meet us. The year was 1980.

It was spring when I met this tall man with his full reddish beard and his great personal warmth. He was seeking to establish a link between his research and a human being with total recall of that time, and I was longing to come to grips with my anxieties and emotional pain. We were a perfect match. We corresponded regularly and, in 1981, I felt strong enough to venture back to the town where I had lost a part of my life. I felt I could retrieve it with help of this gentle man and his wife, Antoinette.

In 1981, the village was shown an exhibit put together by Wolfgang and Miss Kammeier that acquainted young and old with the history of the Jewish community that had once flourished there. There were many pictures and documents they had been able to find through their research and through friends of the old Jewish families. Through the International Search Office in Arolsen, they were able to find where every Jew of Schermbeck was deported and in which concentration camps they had met their deaths. It was the beginning of an emotional reminder to the entire community of what they, as bystanders, had allowed to happen to the Jews.

By 1982, the year of my return, in spite of much opposition, he made it his goal to commemorate the synagogue in Schermbeck that had been destroyed on Kristallnacht.

Wolfgang Bornebusch, Protestant minister and guiding light

With the help of his Presbytery, he was to place a plaque where the synagogue once stood. Working with the burgermeister, he scheduled the dedication for June 22, and arranged to have a rabbi present. Because of my mother's death on June 21, I could not be present. Broken-hearted, I left a taped message to be played in my place and returned to America.

When I visit Germany, and I have gone many times now to Schermbeck and other towns, amazing things continue to happen. At a commemoration ceremony for Kristallnacht held in 1988 at Wolfgang's church, Herman Stricker, a resident of Schermbeck stood before the gathering and stated that as a 15-year-old he was present at Kristallnacht. He then told other community members they also needed to confess to cleanse their souls. I had a chance to embrace him and we shared a special reconciliation. I realized, after all, he had only been a teenager that dreadful night in 1938.

And I will never forget Guy Rammenzweig, a minister from the village of Brunnen, who was also in attendance that night in 1988. Fifty years after Kristallnacht, he came with 25 men and boys to pray for the souls of those who perished. Over the years, each time I returned to Schermbeck I would attend a Sunday service, and each time Wolfgang would welcome me and direct his sermon to special subjects dealing with Christian/Jewish reconciliation. We have done so much work together, yet, because of his gentleness I have been able to address the pain and the horror of the Holocaust which I had unknowingly or knowingly suppressed all of these years. He has introduced me to his friends and people of influence and has given me the opportunity to relive many moments that without him would have been very difficult. Through him I have reacquainted myself with old classmates and their children.

As time went by, I wanted to share my enthusiasm for his work, especially his dedication to the role that a German can play in the healing of tensions and the creation of better understanding not only between Christians and Jews, but, particularly between Germans and Jews. With this in mind, I invited him to be the keynote speaker at our annual Holocaust Remembrance program sponsored by a German chemical corporation based in Pittsburgh. For almost a full year we laid our plans and finally, to my great joy, the evening of Yom Hashoa came and he spoke to a church gathering of 900 Christians and Jews.

Over the years Wolfgang has carried his message to many countries. He has spoken of Christian/Jewish understanding before live audiences on radio talk shows, on TV and in seminars. I love and respect this man and thank him for all he has done.

Can one human being make a difference in the world? I have only to look at Wolfgang Bornebusch. If you drop a stone into a lake at first you don't see much happening. But watch for awhile. There is movement in ripples. Small circles become ever larger ones, spreading out finally to touch . . . what? Hearts? Minds? Maybe souls.

12 | FOREVER A PAINFUL REUNION

Each time I come back to Schermbeck I take a leisurely walk through the town to feed my longing to go home, as well as to relieve the anxiety and apprehension that accompanies the trip. On one recent visit, I had been back for a day and, as I wandered the streets in a ritual I had performed many times before, I saw a well-worn bicycle resting against the wall of the old Overkemping tavern where Schermbeckers still meet, as they did in my grandfather's time.

I knew who the bike belonged to and the sight of it brought a flood of old memories washing over me. I entered the tavern and even though his back was to me, I recognized Willie sitting on a stool. Willie Kupper. Boldly I walked over and tapped him on the shoulder. He spun around slowly, saw me and slid to the floor as we embraced, each shedding tears. Our eyes met and we smiled, temporarily breaking the sadness we both felt. Why the tears? Because we can never forget the events that touched both of our families during those terrible years. A past that is filled with pain for us both.

Whenever I see Willie, I'm reminded of another brave man, a friendly face without a name, who was Opa's friend.

On Kristallnacht when he saw the devastation of all the Jewish homes, and particularly when the bricks were thrown through our windows, he became enraged. He picked up a pitchfork and chased after the Nazis, his terrified mother grabbing at his ankles and trying in vain to hold him back. The children begged for their father to stop, but the Nazis had gone and all was quiet.

Wilhelm Kupper (1938), neighbor and friend to Opa

The second time they came, however, the Nazis were ready for him. They threatened to burn his barn and, reluctantly, the father could only stand idly by and watch. What else could he do? There were many of them and only one of him and, besides, he had his family to worry about. But that didn't stop him from feeling anger and remorse as he listened to the cries and screams emanating from our house next door.

For his actions, the man's family was branded *Judenfreund*, friends of the Jews, which was a label given to people of conscience or those who resisted the Nazi movement of the late 1930s. As a result, the son was called *Judenbengel*, Jew brat, and beaten each time he attended mandatory Hitler Youth meetings. He was made an example to deter others who might consider being sympathetic to our plight. In fact, anyone who showed kindness or assisted Jews was punished by arrest, beatings, or death. This was how the Nazis put fear into the hearts of the German people.

59

Although the Nazis were almost in complete control of Schermbeck, it didn't stop some people from making a stand, however. A plot was hatched to kill the mayor, a clever and ruthless Nazi, but somehow the police got word of it. The five citizens who planned the coup were arrested, questioned, and immediately drafted into the army and sent to the front. Willie, too, was drafted near the end of the war, but he returned safely to work on the family farm. By the grace of God he lived to share these memories with me.

So, this was our connection. This is what brings about the tears and the strong emotions each time we meet. But as we get older, a month, a year further away from the source of our pain and remembering, we focus on the efforts of the good people of Schermbeck. And each time I return I am better able to understand the fear that was instilled into my family's friends and neighbors, and I appreciate even more those who tried against tremendous odds to help.

As long as Willie and I live we will share the pain of the past and console each other in the future. However, I'm envious that although his family lived in fear for many years, at least they lived. Mine was murdered in 1943 against the nightmare landscape of Theresienstadt and Auschwitz and Birkenau and Trawnicky.

13 | EDITH REMEMBERS TOO

It was as if it was yesterday when I had just stepped off the train in Bonn, my heart pounding with anticipation of my rendezvous with my childhood friend, Edith. She was my best friend in Schermbeck all those years ago, and I hadn't seen her since that fateful night when we left. There we stood on the platform. I couldn't believe we were together again, that we should meet once more after 44 years of absence. Neither of us had grown very tall; in fact, I thought she very much resembled the little girl from my memory. We fell into each other's arms, exchanging tight hugs we had saved for each other all these years.

We walked and talked, chattering like the little girls we once were, and seeming to pick up with our friendship as if it were 1938 all over again. "Your hair was brown and wavy," she recalled accurately. "And you had long braids with pretty bows at the end of each," I replied. The conversation continued like that all the way to her home. Soon, we were relaxing on her sofa, retracing our lives and catching up on lost time.

We remembered the time that we washed our dolls' clothes in the creek and that I let her favorite doll's dress drift away. I was unable to retrieve it and, until now, I had been

The author's lifelong friend Edith Venneman as a child (1937)

unable to recall this special time. It seemed like the only memories I had were bad. But Edith comforted me by indicating that she, too, was haunted by the past. She couldn't forget, no matter how hard she tried, the awful events leading up to Kristallnacht. The morning after was the last time we saw each other — a quick good-bye through veiled curtains, she couldn't risk someone seeing her. The war continued, Edith explained, and she and her family survived the air raids and later the occupation of Allied troops. As time passed, she finished her schooling, married and had three sons...all the while wondering where I was and whether I had survived.

It wasn't until 1982, when Edith and her husband, Paul, visited Schermbeck that she knew for sure what had happened to me. She was being served in a local tavern when an old schoolmate, Werner Wink approached their table. "Do you remember Marga Silbermann, our Jewish friend?" he asked. "Of course," Edith replied. "I think she died in one of the concentration camps after they left here." "No, Edith," Werner said with a smile. "She is alive and well. Just last year she was here for a visit." Edith was ecstatic.

I received a letter from Edith in 1983, relating her discovery. In the letter she also described what it had been like for her those many years. The reports in the newspapers of the horrors in the concentration camps and six million Jews being murdered, and she would constantly scan the pages for my face. She could not bear to think that I could have died that way. Ashamed at what the German people allowed the Nazis to do, she was angry, too.

Yet her correspondence wasn't all bad. She described how her three sons had been brought up differently than the youth in our time. They learned to be strong and defend the rights of others. She told them about me and how my family was taken away, she thought, to be killed. But she assured me that her boys understand that something like the Holocaust must never happen again. In her letter she also wished me well and hoped that we would get together one day soon.

Our first reunion was special, but each one since, and there have been many, were almost as exciting and certainly as fulfilling. I am welcomed in her home with pomp and circumstance, and I feel as comfortable speaking to her in English as in German. We spend time reminiscing about the weinstube and weinhaus on the Rhein, which is one of our favorite places. Often, we walk through the wheat fields, forests and countryside, drinking in the scenery and scent of wildflowers on our way to the top of Rolandbogen. The view of the Rhein River from the peak is spectacular, and Edith always seems proud to share with me all of the beautiful places where she has lived.

However, this is a very different Germany than the one I remember. In fact, even today many Jews in Germany do not feel secure. The threat of Neo-Nazism hangs in the air and many German people seem as disinterested in Jews as ever. The comfort level for Jews is still much less than before Hitler's time. And that's a shame. For prior to then Jews lived a comfortable, proud life, assimilated and part of the community. With the Holocaust, however, Jews who have come back after hiding out or being displaced cannot live a truly free life. Many do not list their names in the phone books. They are watched by police during religious services. Schools and Jewish buildings are always under surveillance. I do not foresee a secure Jewish existence in Germany in the distant future, if ever. A recent survey from an article in *Der Spiegel* indicated that 60 percent of Germans would prefer not to live next door to a Jew. Personally, I would never live in Germany again on a permanent basis. I guess it's because America is now my home.

But with friends like Edith there to visit, I will continue to go back. I will remain vigilant against anti-Semitism wherever it raises its ugly head. And I will try to educate people and bridge the gaps that have seemingly widened over time. For now, that's all I can do.

In 1994 Edith and I met in Schermbeck for a day. We drank coffee in a cafe on the main street and commented on how the village was changing. The cobblestone streets are gone and there is an outdoor mall with new trees and wooden benches. Women walk by, carrying their baskets on their arms instead of toting them on bicycles like we remembered. The years we were separated have made our time together now even more precious and rewarding. We often stop in the middle of a conversation and just look at each other, not always comprehending that we are together again. So much has changed in Schermbeck since we lived there, and so much of it has been for the better.

14 | TAKE ME HOME AGAIN

It was when my sister Hilda was battling cancer and I had come to take care of her that for the first time in years we had the opportunity to talk about our lives. To pass the time during her recovery we talked about what we had done, what we had accomplished, our regrets, and our hopes for the future. One day I brought with me some slides of my most recent visit to Lemfoerde and was somewhat surprised when Hilda showed interest. "What is it really like now? Will I ever be well enough to see it again?" she asked.

Medical intervention and self-determination allowed my sister to get well enough that we began to think seriously about taking a trip together. For a year I planned our return and now it was about to become a reality. I wondered how she would react, and how I would respond as well.

The train came to a stop and I was able to read the sign on the station wall that read Lemfoerde. The year was 1986 and I had brought my sister, Hilda, back home to the place where we were born. We gathered our bags and stepped onto the platform; for her it was the first time back in Lemfoerde since we escaped with the clothes on our back.

One of Hilda's childhood friends, Annie, met us and they greeted each other warmly. We drove through the town and even though most of the homes on the main street were still standing, the place didn't quite look the same. As we passed the old hotel, Hilda recalled breaking a window there once playing ball with our brothers. Later we called on some old friends, and it seemed to me rather touching that each one desperately tried to remember stories from our common past that would include us and make us feel welcome. Through it all, Hilda seemed calm, almost at ease with her return. On the surface, at least, it appeared nothing like my apprehensive first visit.

We had a room reserved for one night at Hohlmeyer's Hotel and, upon entering, we noticed that very little had changed. A simple light fixture hung from the ceiling in the lobby, its silk fringe faded and worn. Through the doorway I could see the bar with wooden planks for tables and chairs to match. The polished brass handle of the beer tap twinkled in the dim light, and for a moment I could almost envision my father and his friends drinking there, sharing boisterous conversation and laughter.

Our room upstairs was primitive by modern standards, but we found it enchanting. There was a sink in the corner, two wicker chairs, frayed and sagging, and a comfortable bed. But we had a heavy feather

Together, for now. From left, the author's siblings: Manfred, Hilda and Herbert, 1928.

comforter, perfect for a cozy night's sleep in the cool, fall air. As Hilda readied for bed, she looked out the window and commented how the village had not changed very much. She called me to her side and pointed to the part of the street where our house had been, and I was glad she had noticed. I'm sure we both slept well, dreaming of a different Lemfoerde, an unspoiled village, untouched by the evil of war — a nice place to grow up.

In the morning our friends drove us to the cemetery where our father and other family members lie buried. Located in the middle of farm land, it is neat and well cared for and complements the wheat fields dotted with poppies and cornflowers. Adelsheimers and Silbermanns have been laid to rest there since the 17th century — old stones chiseled in Hebrew mark their graves. Weathered and covered with moss, the crude headstones and inscriptions reminded us that we had once been an integral part of this community.

Once back in Lemfoerde, Hilda and I linked arms like schoolmates and walked through town trying to recall various landmarks and touchstones with our youth. She pointed out the pump house where our father had been a volunteer fireman and a building of stucco and beam, now a gift shop, which had once been her school. Further along main street we stopped in front of a large, white house where Hilda was sure Opa was born. I recognized several places myself, but I was enjoying seeing Lemfoerde again for the first time, this time through my sister's eyes.

As the shadows began to lengthen, the bell in the big church around the bend began to gong, drowning out our conversation. Over the din, Hilda pointed down the road to a house now orange in the fading sunlight. She was sure it had

once been a synagogue. I couldn't be
certain, but I believe she was right. I
Outside our home in Lemfoerde
before the Kristallnacht
was pleasantly surprised by her revelation and, at the same
time, I was somewhat shocked that I had missed it.

Our day was coming to an end and I hoped with all my
heart that it was as fulfilling and gratifying for Hilda as it had
been for me. Being older, surely she had more vivid memories
than me. But was it what she had expected? Did the people
and places have the same effect on her as they did me? For my
part, I believe it did. I think it was a great gift for her to be well
and able to return to share her memories, even if only with
me.

15 | THESE STORIES MUST BE TOLD

I had met Andrea Kammeier in 1982 when she interviewed me for a story she was writing about my family in Schermbeck. She was researching the history of the Jewish community of Schermbeck and was better acquainted with the facts than I would ever be — but, nonetheless, she wanted my input.

I was grateful for all that she had uncovered about German Jews and I admired her for the dedication and effort she had put into the project. We soon developed a warm friendship, and now she wanted me to meet her Oma. On a return to my roots, I decided to visit her.

Upon reaching their home, I found a vegetable patch that reminded me of the one in Opa's garden. I saw Andrea and her grandmother sitting on the porch, and they waved for me to join them. Distant church bells began to chime as Andrea got up to greet me. I exchanged pleasantries with her grandmother, and she shared some of her memories from the past. I had many questions about the destruction of the Schermbeck synagogue which had stood just a few feet away from where we were standing, and I hoped that Frau Kammeier could recall how the events had taken place.

Many of the Jewish homes and Andrea Kammeier in Schermbeck (1996) living quarters had been destroyed and their contents thrown into the streets and surrounding gardens, and the synagogue was one of the few places remaining untouched. The plunder and destruction of our modest house of worship began about midday on December 10th. After the Nazis' henchmen pitched the shingles off the roof they tried to collapse the framework by tying a rope to a tree in the garden of Wilhelm Hoppuns, who happened to be my grandmother's father. But he did not allow this to happen, and the building was saved. Much later, however, the front wall of the synagogue was damaged and, because of the danger, it was torn down completely. The remaining walls were dismantled after the war, leaving only those with memories of the building to testify that it even existed.

She told me about that and other events from the war, which made her very sad. I listened intently as she recounted a heavy attack on the village even though it held no strategic value. The destruction was so widespread that she said she could not even find a spoon in the rubble. Her demeanor turned from sadness to pride, however, when she related how she refused to greet anyone with a Heil Hitler. She also said that she did not remember when the few remaining Jews were taken from their homes in 1941 and deported. However, she had heard through rumors from soldiers that her neighbors were taken to the train station and on their way to the concentration camps in the east were shot. She was glad I was not one of them.

And that's the way it went for many Germans and German-Jews alike. Both of my brothers overcame the odds and escaped the Nazis, but unfortunately not without further pain. In fact, Herbert was sentenced to hard labor on the Isle of Man in England because he had lost his papers. Later, he was shipped to Australia to be interned there until the end of the war. I would not see him again until our joyous reunion in 1946. Manfred also experienced good and bad times while trying to reunite with our family. He remained in England during the war, working at a munitions plant, and later was recognized for his efforts in possibly shortening the war. Ironically, he had been a student in Frankfurt prior to the war and he had spied the Germans burying huge petrol tanks on the outskirts of the city, which would later be used in preparation for their invasions. He provided the information to the Ministry of War Department, which then targeted the gas reserves for bombing. Unfortunately, Manfred lived only to the age of 35, another life cut short as a result of the Holocaust.

Over the course of my lifetime I have met many heroes and heroines. Some have done difficult, nearly impossible things, and I find their motivation inspiring. Such is the case with Johanna Eichmann. We were first introduced in 1988 when a young teacher I knew arranged for me to speak to her class at a school gymnasium. My talk completed, I was suddenly aware that Johanna had been in the back of the room throughout my entire program. She came forward and introduced herself as the director of the convent. From the start I was moved by her gentle ways and outward sincerity. I realized immediately that she was an extraordinary person, a person who had witnessed life from the depths of fear to the pinnacle of success.

Johanna had been loved and respected during her 27 years as director as well as in the community of nuns. She has devoted her energy, her heart and mind to a cause that has consumed her and endeared her to people throughout the entire region. Many have benefited from her dedication and commitment to helping others, and we are forever grateful for all she has done and continues to do. In addition, her knowledge of religion, history and the Holocaust is boundless, and I believe she has been chosen to deliver the message for all who want the world to be a better place.

Johanna was born Ruth Rosenthal in Nordhine, Westfalen. She was raised in a Jewish household and practiced Judaism, the religion of her mother, but because Jews were ostracized and harassed in the 1930s, she was later baptized as a Catholic. As a student in the Ursuline gymnasium, Ruth was taught by nuns and accepted as a Christian until a Nazi director discovered her deception and she was expelled. Fortunately, there were still some commercial schools available that she could attend. At the age of sixteen she went to Berlin, took an examination to become an interpreter and, subsequently, in 1943 she attended the Berlitz School.

Until this time, the Nazis were not too hard on families of Jewish women married to non-Jews, and their children, but in 1944 all of those in Westphalia were rounded up and arrested. Ruth was still in Berlin and escaped their wrath, but one can only wonder what might have happened had she been home at that time. In March of 1945 with the Allied armies approaching, many Jewish women were taken and gassed, and though her father tried to convince her to hide from the Gestapo, Ruth would not leave Berlin. She joined many of the half-Jews who were then put to forced labor in factories, toiling throughout the day and waiting out the air raids at night. By May, Berlin was in ruins and occupied by Russian soldiers who had advanced from the east. With luck, Ruth was able to reach the American occupied zone and finally felt free for the first time in years.

With the end of the war, Ruth returned to complete her studies at Muenster and Toulouse as she pursued an education in journalism. Through it all she never forgot the compassion and kindness of the Ursuline nuns. As a result, she decided to enter the convent and become a nun, Schwester Johanna. Within time she became the director, but her story doesn't stop there. For under the cloistered exterior of a nun beat the heart of a Jew, a Jew who could not forget the millions murdered because of their religious affiliation. She had decided that those human beings, beautiful people like her grandfather, must be remembered.

Working with a group of young men and women, Sister Johanna helped form a group to research artifacts of the once active Jewish community of Dorsten in Westfalia. Their dream was to create a museum that one day would teach about Jewish religion, culture and history to Germans and anyone else

who came through the doors. In
the process, the group wrote seven
books entitled *Dorsten untern*

Hakenkreuz (Dorsten Under the Swastika), which represents a
complete history of the Jewish community from the time prior
to Nazi take-over and continuing until deportation and death.

Because the history of the Holocaust is taught in Germany and the people are aware of all that happened during
that terrible time, Johanna and her group felt that a museum
might be a real possibility. They petitioned the town officers
and mayor with their idea and discovered that a building was
about to be demolished — so they could have it for free. Suddenly a dream was about to become a reality. With hard work
and a lot of effort, they could reclaim the razed building as
their monument to the past. There would be rooms to house
books, cases to display artifacts as they had envisioned, and a
special area for lectures. It would have temperature control,
an elevator and even special lighting. But that wasn't all. Behind the building there would be a garden for quiet reflection

and meditation. Today, the Judisches Museum Westfalen at the center of town displays a commemorative pillar cast by Schwester Paula, Tisa von der Schulenburg, a contributing member of the group.

When the museum opened in 1992, the Minister-praesident Nordrhein-Westfalen was the keynote speaker. A group of Israelis from Dorsten's adopted-sister city of Hod Hasharon were in attendance as the rabbi delivered his blessing, affixing a mesuza to its entrance. I was also invited to attend as a charter member from the United States, and I was honored to be included in this special group of people. As Schwester Johanna spoke, a reverent hush came over the crowd. This woman, born a Jew and now a driving force of the Catholic church, was looked upon as a true representative of God — a person who stood for goodness, even though she had witnessed so much evil in her life. I was proud to be her friend.

16 | THE GOOD NEIGHBOR

As I was growing up in America my family often talked about the elderly woman who used to milk Opa's cows every day. They recalled how she cared for the cows and that there was so much milk that they often gave it away to poor people in the area. She spent a great deal of time with our family in the times before Germany changed forever. We wondered what had happened to her.

Mother remembered that when the Nuremburg Laws went into effect in 1935, we were no longer permitted to employ Christian help. It was then that the milkmaid had to stop milking our cows. She was well liked and a good worker, and she would be missed. It meant that my grandfather could no longer retain milk cows and cattle, but more unfortunately, the maid's leaving meant that there wouldn't be any surplus of milk for the poor.

Soon after the milkmaid left, the lone cow she owned became ill and, in the absence of a veterinarian, my Opa put the animal to sleep. Then, as a reward for her years of service, Opa replaced it with a healthy cow from his pasture. I'm sure it brought him more satisfaction than any of the cows he had sold off.

A forgotten name, but never a forgotten face. The milkmaid.

I often thought about that woman. Where did life take her? What did she look like now? Was she married, and did she have children?

In 1992 Reverend Bornebusch introduced me to an elderly couple, who had said they would like to meet me. A visit was arranged, introductions made, and I settled in at their modest home to hear what they had to say. To my delight, the woman began telling me that Opa had given her mother a cow to replace the one that had died. She related how her mother had worked for years milking cows for my family. It was yet another discovery from the graveyard of my past.

After I left that day, I smiled at the discovery of a long-lost person from my past. It was good to meet the milkmaid's daughter who looked so much like her mother when she was young. It was as if I was four years old again, seeing that face again, and the feeling was warm and comforting. Today, I have a picture of the milkmaid that her daughter handed to me as I left, and I'll always remember her squeezing my hand with the same love and tenderness I imagined her mother had reserved for her favorite cows.

17 | HOPE FOR THE FUTURE

It was November in the Rheinland, cold and dark and reminiscent of an earlier time that I often wish I wouldn't remember. I was in Dinslaken to commemorate Kristallnacht, their night of terror, destruction and pain, fifty years later.

My mother had worked for a wealthy Jewish family here, and it was at the Jewish orphanage that she witnessedone of her saddest memories of the Holocaust. Children were taken from the orphanage and placed in haywagons and deported, leading them most likely to their deaths.

It was 1988 and there would be a memorial service for the victims this night. The crowd grew to more than 1,500 and I couldn't help but wonder where all of these people were when the children were put into a hay wagon and eventually marched to their death, but I didn't dwell on that. Instead, I watched as votive candles were lit and distributed along with placards with the names of the orphans who perished.

The procession began and we walked silently in the chilled night air, the steam from our breath rising in wisps that looked like tiny ghosts from the past. No one spoke, their faces somber, as we made our way to the Catholic church. I walked with Reverend Bornebusch, his parents and my friends who came all the way from my hometown, Pittsburgh. As I looked around, again I was filled with questions: Do they feel compassion for the wrongs done to Jews? Do they have guilt? Sadness? Maybe even anger? It seemed to me that whatever they may be feeling and thinking, that their presence in such numbers showed that they do not deny what happened here, and that it was wrong.

From behind the procession came a noise that roused me from my thoughts. It was a sound I hadn't heard since my childhood — the uneven rattle and creak of a wagon rolling over cobblestone streets. The melancholy sound of the wheels drew me near, and I could see that the wagon was being pulled by men, and that more men, these with lanterns, walked along-side. Behind them were young people with the orphan's names on placards.

The procession finally came to a halt outside the church, and the group, as if having one collective set of eyes, watched as the wagon slowly passed by. People began to enter the build-ing and I suddenly found myself behind the wagon, which was empty, a reminder of those who lost their lives that fate-ful night. I then noticed for the first time a cross standing three stories tall over the group. I clutched the post of the wagon, and for a moment, the children were there, sitting and standing with me, sharing a painful reunion.

Overcome with grief, I strained to gain my composure. As I looked into the darkness, out of the corner of my eye I saw a little girl riding on her father's shoulders. She had a piece of cardboard under her arm and as her father set her down be-side me, I could read what she had written: "Why did those children suffer so? Let us be friends with the Jews." Through tears of joy I could also see drawings of little children she had made to accompany her sage message.

So young, yet so knowing.
Henrike Sagel.

I bent down closer to her, as if I might gain some greater insight from this tiny angel. "I am a Jew," I said. "And I was just about your age when Kristallnacht took place." I told her about my mother and how she was arrested and taken to the orphanage which had been emptied the day before. The next thing I knew, we were all kneeling down together, her father and mother, the child and I. We embraced each other and prayed. I was moved to tears; we all were.

I asked the child, whose name was Henrike, if I could take her artwork back to America with me, and she smiled. We exchanged addresses and went into the church to participate in the solemn memorial service for the souls of our murdered brothers and sisters.

Henrike was only eight years old, the child of ministers, mother and father both. She had a brother and older sister and several pets. And now I was included in her circle of friends.

We have become close and correspond to this day, and I believe our chance encounter has had a great impact on us both — I feel a more profound hope for the future, while through me Henrike has experienced a unique connection with the past.

I have returned several times to Dinslaken to see Henrike and, on one visit, I even lectured to her class. Some of the students wore patches on their shirts or jackets, an emblem showing a crushed swastika and a fist that crushed it. The slogan underneath read *Gegen Nazis*, Against Nazis.

In 1991 plans were formulated to build a monument in memory of the orphans of Dinslaken and for all of those who had perished in the Holocaust. Henrike wrote that she was very excited about it, especially because it was her art teacher who had submitted the rendering for its creation. Today, a bronze cast hay wagon, bronzed shoes, purses and other artifacts stand at that sight in Dinslaken. The orphans are no longer just numbers. Their names are etched in bronze covering a large portion of the monument, a fitting reminder of an enormous tragedy that should never have occurred, and hopefully never will again.

I visited the monument with Henrike and, as we stood there silently, I was reminded of the first time we had met. She had given me such hope, and even now inspiration for a bright future. I was filled with pride at having added to her already strong belief in humane treatment for all people and respect for their rights. I saw a young woman on her way to becoming a leader in the community, and a voice of reason for generations of Germans to come.

It has been nine years since our first meeting. Time has made her even more mature, and through her, time has given me hope for a better future. I wonder, will my young friend make a difference? Will I make a difference? Will you?

EPILOGUE

I once read a quote by Thomas Campbell that said, "To live in the hearts of those we leave behind is truly not to die." The full realization of what that quote means came to me shortly after I returned to Schermbeck the first time. It became clear to me that I had a mission, a mission to reclaim my past and memorialize those who had their future cut short.

With the help of Reverend Bornebusch, I began to deal with the emotional barriers that kept me from revisiting my past. I was able to move ahead by going back, back to the place where it all began. No longer would I be afraid of the memories and places. I had nothing to fear and, in fact, resurrecting their good names was a fitting revenge against all those who hate. Through my words, written and spoken, I can bring back their lives, their dignity, their accomplishments and love for one another that meant so much to them and that influence my life to this very day.

By 1980, Holocaust survivors began to speak up and memorial centers had begun to appear in most U.S. cities. The world had seen the movie "Holocaust," and it raised aware-

Built in the 19th century, the Schermbeck synagogue was destroyed during the Kristallnacht of November 9–10, 1938

ness among people that allowed those of us who could speak out to do so without hesitation. It was then that I began to tell my story to anyone who would listen. I spoke in schools and meetings at churches and clubs. I attended every workshop, conference, and public gathering that provided information. I was hungry for knowledge about survivors who had suffered in the concentration camps, who were hidden by non-Jewish families, and who had lived in the Warsaw ghetto.

My knowledge base broadened considerably more after several trips to Schermbeck. At large gatherings or face-to-face with individuals, I questioned people who lived through the Holocaust. I felt privileged to share such painful memories, things that I was often asked to verify and speak about — all part of my life as a survivor. I spoke out in support of the Christian Holocaust work that ministers and teachers were doing. It was vitally important to me that I do this and, at the same time, fulfill my obligations to keep the memory of the

Holocaust victims alive.

In 1992 I began to develop a large network of clergy and educators, many who attended a workshop Wolfgang Bornebusch created called "From Distrust to Knowing." This network, in turn, has allowed me to lecture to all levels of school children when I visit Germany and hopefully make the period of the Holocaust come to life for them. They are able to ask questions of a Jew who survived and understand better what that time in history was about.

I continue to teach out of the conviction that future generations must remember this tragedy and what it has meant to those of us who survived and lived to talk about it. It has not always been easy, but during my struggles so many good things have happened. I rekindled relationships with long-lost friends and made new friends that will last a lifetime. But my work is not done.

During 1994 while in Berlin I was able to film a documentary on the Holocaust period, including a scene in Koerner Park where I once played and later was banished for being a Jew. It was also through the efforts of the Jewish Community Center in Berlin that I was able to contact a second cousin, Gerhard Zadek, and we were reunited. He shared stories of his escape to England during the war and some things I had forgotten about our twin cousins who had perished. I also had the opportunity to lecture and live on the premises at the Ursuline Convent at the behest of its director, sister Johanna Eichmann of the Ursuline Order. I was a charter member of the museum since its opening in 1992 and was honored that they had created a Jewish museum, an unusual and wonderful thing for such a small group.

So I continue to dedicate my life to this cause. Not only

to speak for my family, but to incorporate all of the victims of the Holocaust and pray for their peace in eternity. I hope to make a difference, and I firmly believe that my efforts to raise awareness and educate people about this tragic event will create greater understanding and tolerance in the treatment of other human beings.

The culmination of all my life experiences in traveling back to my village has brought me to a point in my life where I want to burst with stories, discoveries, and knowledge that just cannot die with me. I will only be fulfilled when I have reached the consciousness of all people who were not aware of the Holocaust, the annihilation of millions that left this world a poorer place. In memory of those who died and their families that must live on, I hope to build bridges to the future so that we may walk across them together.

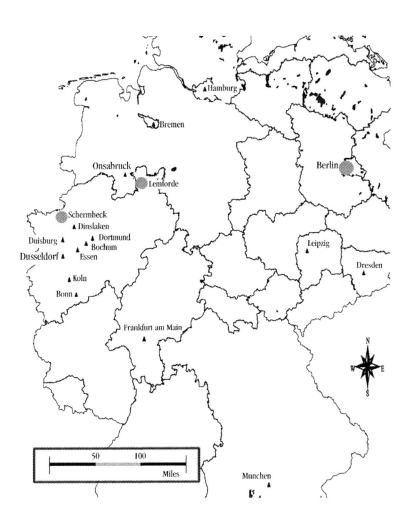

A map of Germany that highlights cities
and areas referred to within the text.

TIMELINE OF THE HOLOCAUST PERIOD

1933

January 30   Adolf Hitler is appointed Chancellor of Germany.

March 22   Dachau concentration camp opens.

April 1   Widespread boycott of Jewish shops and businesses.

April 7   Jews are barred from holding civil service, university and state positions.

1934

August 2   Hitler proclaims himself *Fuhrer und Reichskanzler* (Leader and Reich Chancellor) and armed forces must now swear allegiance to him.

1935

September 15 The anti-Semitic Nuremburg Laws are enacted.

1936

March 3   Jewish doctors are barred from practicing medicine in German institutions.

October 25   Hitler and Mussolini agree to form the Berlin-Rome Axis.

1937

July 15   Buchenwald concentration camp opens.

1938

March 13   Under the Anschluss, all anti-Semitic decrees immediately apply in Austria.

July 6   The Evian Conference on the problem of Jewish refugees is held in France.

September 30   Great Britain and France agree at the Munich Conference to German occupation of the Sudetenland, previously western Czecho-slovakia.

October 5   At the request of Swiss authorities, Germans mark all Jewish passports with a "J" to restrict Jews from immigrating to Switzerland.

October 28   Approximately 17,000 Polish Jews living in Germany are expelled. Poland refuses to admit them and 8,000 are stranded in the frontier village of Zbaszyn.

November   Kristallnacht and anti-Jewish pogroms are
9–10   carried out in Germany, Austria and Sudetenland.

November 12   A decree is passed in Germany to transfer all retail businesses to Aryan hands.

November 15 All Jewish pupils are expelled from German
             schools.

1939

March 15   Nazi Germany invades and occupies Czecho-
             slovakia.
May 13   The American vessel S.S. St. Louis leaves
             Hamburg for Cuba carrying 900 Jewish
             passengers.
September 1 Nazi Germany invades Poland, which signals
             the beginning of World War II.

1940

April 9   Nazi Germany invades Denmark and Norway.
April 30   Hitler creates the first major Jewish ghetto in
             Lodz, Poland.
May 10   Nazi Germany invades the Netherlands,
             Belgium, Luxembourg and France.

1941

April 6   Nazi Germany invades Yugoslavia and Greece.
June 22   Nazi Germany invades the Soviet Union,
             and mobile killing squads known as *Einsatz-
             gruppen* begin mass shootings of Jews,
             gypsies, and Communists in the east.
September 23 Auschwitz is the first site of experimental
             gassing.
December 11 Nazi Germany declares war on the United
             States of America.

	1942
March 1	Mass gassings of Jews begin at Auschwitz, where 1.1 million Jews are executed by 1944.
April 1	Mass gassings begin at Sobibor, Belzec and Treblinka, where 1.5 million Jews are executed by late 1943.
	1945
May 7	Nazi Germany surrenders to the Allied forces as the war in Europe ends.

1945-47

Displaced Person (D.P.) camps are set up by the U.S. Army and the Red Cross to help refugees get food, shelter, and medical attention, as well as locate lost family members.

1948

The United States passes the Displaced Persons Act, allowing Jewish and non-Jewish war refugees to enter the United States in massive numbers.

REFERENCES AND SUGGESTED READINGS

Auerbacher, I. (1993). *I Am a Star. Child of the Holocaust.* Puffin Books: New York.

Campbell, T. (c. 1800). "Hallowed Ground."

Judischer Frontsoldaten (A Book of Commemoration. The Jewish Soldiers who Fought at the Front for Their Country). Druck, Lessman: Hamburg, Germany. 1932.

Frank, A. (1958). *Diary of Anne Frank.* Simon & Schuster, Inc.: New York.

Gross, L. (1982). *The Last Jews in Berlin.* Simon & Schuster: New York.

Klein, G.W. (1957). *All But My Life.* Hill and Wang: New York.

Lipstadt, D. (1993). *Denying the Holocaust: The Growing Assault on Truth and Memory.* The Free Press, Division of Macmillan, Inc.: New York.

Mates, C. (1993). *Daniel's Story.* Scholastic, Inc.: New York.

Merty, B. (1982). *Understanding the Holocaust.* J. Western Walsh: Portland, ME.

Tenbrook, R.H. *Zeiten und Menschen (Times and People).* Schoeningh Schroedel and Kurt Kluxen.

Wiesel, E. (1928), *Night.* Bantam: New York

ABOUT
THE AUTHOR

Marga Silbermann Randall is a Holocaust survivor who was born in
Lemforde, Germany in 1930. She fled
to America with her immediate family
in 1941, where she learned to speak English and later attained U.S. citizenship.
She married, had a family, and worked
most of her life in the public sector.
After 45 years, Marga returned to her
home town in Germany to regain her

PHOTO: ROCKY RACO

past, and since 1981 she has devoted her life to educating
people about the Holocaust. She has made hundreds
of presentations at universities, public and private schools,
conducted Holocaust workshops and seminars, and spoken
to community and civic organizations. She has written and
lectured on the subject of the Holocaust, produced a documentary for National Public Television, and has been
interviewed for and featured on television and radio.
This is her first book.

Remarkable Praise for
How Beautiful We Once Were

"Because of Marga Randall and her telling biography, more and more members of my congregation are able to face the history of the Jews in Germany and in Schermbeck, especially the era of the Third Reich."

Pastor Wolfgang Bornebush
St. Georgekirche
Shermbeck, Germany

"Marga Randall, in spite of the horrible memories, has had the strength to visit Germany…. Step by step she has been able to start a conversation, even with the old German generation, that has proved to be very valuable. Marga Randall's mission is so important."

Ignatz Bubis
President
Jewish Council
Frankfurt, Germany

"We should be grateful to Marga Randall for this contribution to our further understanding of evil and heroic deeds of this sad period of history."

Howard M. Rieger
President
United Jewish Federation